C&IM

CHICAGO & ILLINOIS MIDLAND

CHICAGO & ILLINOIS MIDLAND RAILWAY
In Color

BY

RYAN CRAWFORD AND JAMES E. LEWNARD

Copyright © 2009
Morning Sun Books, Inc.

All rights reserved. This book may not be reproduced in part or in whole without written permission from the publisher, except in the case of brief quotations or reproductions of the cover for the purposes of review.

To access our full library *In Color* visit us at
www.morningsunbooks.com

Published by
Morning Sun Books, Inc.
9 Pheasant Lane
Scotch Plains, NJ 07076
Printed in Korea

Library of Congress
Catalog Card No. 2009924255

First Printing
ISBN 1-58248-271-3

ROBERT J. YANOSEY, President

ACKNOWLEDGEMENTS

This book would not be possible without the kind and gracious assistance of the following people. Jim and Ryan would like to thank:
- All of the wonderful C&IM employees who answered all of our questions and treated us like friends throughout the years.
- Richard Wallin, who has enthusiastically supported our project.
- C&IM conductors Gene Anderson and Dallas Stout, who took time out of their busy schedules to explain the operations of the railroad in detail. These gentlemen spent hours looking at slides and provided their personal employee time books for research and verification of information.
- Retired engineer Joe Myerscough for explaining the steam operations on the railroad.
- Engineers Lynn Pulley and Kathy Guy for explaining the post 1970's diesel operations.
- C&IM carmen Wayne Books and Billy Williams for explaining locomotive repainting and providing insight about the freight car fleet.
- Gary Helling for editing photos and editing several photo captions.
- Joe Lewnard, for editing photos.
- Chris Kunz for helping pick up and deliver slides.
- Trey Kunz for explaining the B&O's Springfield area operations during the 1980's.
- Tom Ratsch for allowing us to use his collection of C&IM time tables.
- Bob Yanosey for publishing this book and providing a number of wonderful slides.

The following photographers generously shared their work: Larry Anglund, Roger Bee, C&IM Chapter NRHS, Joe Collias, Hal Collins, Terry Cook, James DuBose, Paul Fries, Gary Helling, Roger A. Holmes, Ed Johnson, John & Roger Kujawa, Trey Kunz, Merlyn Lauber, Joe Lewnard, Scott Muskopf, Martha Smith, Bill Raia, Tom Ratsch, Steve Rippeteau, Richard Wallin, Richard Ward, Don Woodworth and Bob Yanosey.

Thank you also to the C&IM Chapter of the National Railway Historical Society, managers of the Chatham Railway Museum. The museum is located at 100 N. State Street, Chatham, Illinois, in the former GM&O Depot, owned by the Village of Chatham. Many of the details in the photo captions were checked for accuracy with C&IM railroad documents that were graciously provided by the society.

Ryan Crawford would like to thank the following people for making this book a success. Thanks go to:
- My wife Jennifer and daughters Jessica, Katie and Kristen, for allowing me to have a "one track mind" throughout this project.
- My father Dan, for taking me on weekend trips to the Diesel Shop and on railfan excursions following C&IM trains during my younger years, which allowed me to learn all that I could about the Midland operations and its exotic diesel fleet.
- Jim Lewnard, a best friend and co-author, for teaching me more than I thought possible about railroading in general, and about how the Midland fit into the U.S. railway operating scheme.

LEFT and PAGE 1 - Darkness has fallen upon SD38-2's #71 and 72 sitting next to the Diesel Shop at Springfield awaiting a call to duty on September 18, 1990. *(Scott Muskopf)*

CHICAGO & ILLINOIS MIDLAND RAILWAY *In Color*

On a foggy May 1st in 1983, Chicago & Illinois Midland RS1325 31 coupled on to a lone caboose near the yard office at Shops Yard, pumped up the air, and departed quickly. Rolling north, the little train rattled over the ICG diamonds at Ridgely Tower, rounded a curve, and disappeared into the hilly terrain to the east of the Illinois State Fairgrounds. To many rail-oriented observers, the Chicago & Illinois Midland was as mysterious as the one engine caboose hop that ran north from Springfield that foggy day. During the 1980's it often appeared that the railroad had very little business and rarely ran a train, at least not on the southern half of the line. The coal trains that once ran north from the mines near Taylorville to Havana and Powerton had disappeared. Many small businesses no longer shipped carload freight over the C&IM. Surely a railroad could not survive hauling cabooses up and down the mainline.

In 1980 Richard Wallin, Paul H. Stringham, and John Szwajkart ended their superb history of the Chicago & Illinois Midland, wondering what the future might hold for this small railroad that hauled coal in a nation that was in the midst of an energy crisis.

"C&IM's future hangs in a balance which will eventually be tipped by political and economic considerations which the railroad and its owner, Commonwealth Edison, may have little or no control over." Yet they concluded that the C&IM would continue to serve the basic purpose for which it was founded: providing "a link in the process of converting coal to electricity." Their prediction was accurate. Unlike many railroads of a similar size that have disappeared in recent time, the C&IM survived. In 2009, the Illinois and Midland Railroad, which took over the operations of the C&IM in 1996, carries on the essential mission: hauling coal for generating electricity. Coal-laden trains still roll on the mainline from Pekin through Springfield to Kincaid to serve three large generating stations.

The following work will explore the "mystery" of the C&IM's operations from the end of World War II until the sale of the railroad in February of 1996. It will also describe the efforts of the railroad to provide essential service to its customers, especially in the rapidly changing economic circumstances of the 1980's and 1990's. The essence of the story is told in the photo captions.

We are indebted to the work of Richard Wallin, Paul Stringham, and John Szwajkart for providing the historical basis for our book. Hopefully it will help complete the narration of the C&IM's history that they told so well. The historical data in the captions was verified using railroad documents provided by the Chicago and Illinois Midland Chapter of the National Railway Historical Society, historical artifacts in the authors' collections, and timebooks of retired engineers and conductors. We interviewed many retired C&IM employees and asked them to view the pictures chosen for the book. The photo sessions stimulated many interesting discussions. Many of the captions reflect their collective memories of the events of the last forty years of the railroad's operations. Unfortunately, we could not incorporate all of the stories that they shared.

Ryan Crawford and James E. Lewnard, January 27, 2009

CHICAGO & ILLINOIS MIDLAND RAILWAY *In Color*

Hidden among the many notations the Chicago & Illinois Midland's dispatcher made in his record book each day is a short message: " 600PM, August 14th 1945, Japan accepts unconditional surrender." Two days later, another note appears: "All mines idle 8/15 & 16 celebrating VJ day." Certainly the railroad's employees must have paused to celebrate VJ Day. The war was over. The nation rejoiced, gave thanks, cried, and hoped for a future freed from conflict and fear. Everyone hoped for the safe return of the men and women who helped defeat the Axis powers. And everyone hoped that their lives could return to normal pursuits and tasks.

Normal for the men and women of the C&IM meant hauling coal. At the height of the war they hauled an average of 600 loads a day. On April 25, 1944, they hauled 798 loads.

Every business day mine runs left Taylorville to switch the coal mines on the southern end of the railroad. Sturdy 2-10-2's pulled the loads and set the empties. The Peabody coal mines at Kincaid, Tovey, Langleyville, and Hewittville could produce up to 300 loads a day. Connecting roads at Havana and Pekin delivered still more coal to feed Commonwealth Edison's hungry power plants. Each day road crews at Taylorville and Springfield mounted more sturdy 2-10-2's to assemble coal laden cars into 50 to 60 car trains and haul them north.

As the coal trains rolled north, switch crews with solid 0-8-0's shuffled more coal loads and "high" cars at Taylorville and Shops into the merchandise trains. On the mainline, fast 700 series 2-10-2's moved the 40 series merchandise trains at speeds approaching sixty though the flat Illinois cornfields. Dodging in between the time freights and coal trains were locals #22/23, serving local businesses and delivering less than car load freight to the stations along the line.

Except for a brief five month pause in mid-1945, two passenger trains ran each way daily from Springfield to Pekin. Rare was the day when a C&IM passenger train had more than a railway post office car and a coach. The passenger trains served small, rural communities. There was little need for dining or parlor cars. But the crews were friendly, and their service helped keep the little towns connected to the rest of the state.

Assisting the hard working train crews in the task of keeping the railroad moving was a small army of agents, clerks, shopmen, and trackworkers. Together they shared in the small victories of the War on the home front. In late 1945 the employees of the C&IM had every reason to believe that the task of hauling the coal and merchandise would continue for years to come. The nation's renewed prosperity in a peaceful world would certainly keep the railroad healthy and strong. The Depression was over and the world needed American goods to recover and rebuild. Certainly their best customer and owner, Commonwealth Edison, would keep the trains full of coal.

The C&IM of 1945 was in a sense a very young railroad. The modern C&IM was created in 1926 when Commonwealth Edison purchased the Pekin to Springfield mainline of the Chicago, Peoria, & St. Louis. Trackage rights were secured over the Illinois Central from Springfield to Cimic Illinois, allowing access to the original C&IM, which extended from Cimic east to Taylorville. With generous funding from Commonwealth Edison the "new" C&IM rebuilt the line north of Springfield to accommodate a significant increase in tonnage. Long term plans included the creation of a new coal transfer plant on the Illinois River at Havana. When the purchase was negotiated, it was decided that part of the right-of-way would be expanded to allow the construction of a parallel electric transmission system. Commonwealth Edison then constructed a new power plant just south of Pekin in 1928. The coal for the new Powerton facility came from the Peabody mines east of Cimic as well as from mines on other railroads in southern Illinois.

But in another sense the C&IM of 1945 was one of the older railroads of Illinois. The earliest component of the expanded Chicago & Illinois Midland began life as the Illinois River Railroad. Construction began at Pekin in the summer of 1859. By August of 1860 the rails extended through Havana to Virginia, Illinois. The second component of the modern C&IM began operations as the Springfield and Northwestern, which initiated service from Havana to Springfield in 1874. In 1881 the rapidly expanding Wabash system gained control of the two roads, which also included 25% ownership of the newly-formed Peoria and Pekin Union. Although neither of these railroads had generated substantial business, the Wabash wanted to gain access to Peoria, which the two roads could provide. Unfortunately, the Wabash had financially extended itself far too quickly. Control of the two small roads was surrendered in 1887 to a new company, the Chicago, Peoria, & St. Louis, which through consolidations and leases actually assembled a railroad extending from Peoria to East St. Louis, Illinois.

At the same time that the Wabash's attempt to expand its empire across central Illinois was unraveling, the citizens of Pawnee, a small village 13 miles southeast of Springfield, decided that their community needed to be connected to Illinois's growing rail network. Greatly disappointed by the St. Louis & Chicago Railroad's decision to build its new line to the west of their thriving community, the citizens of Pawnee built their own railroad. Operations began in 1888 between

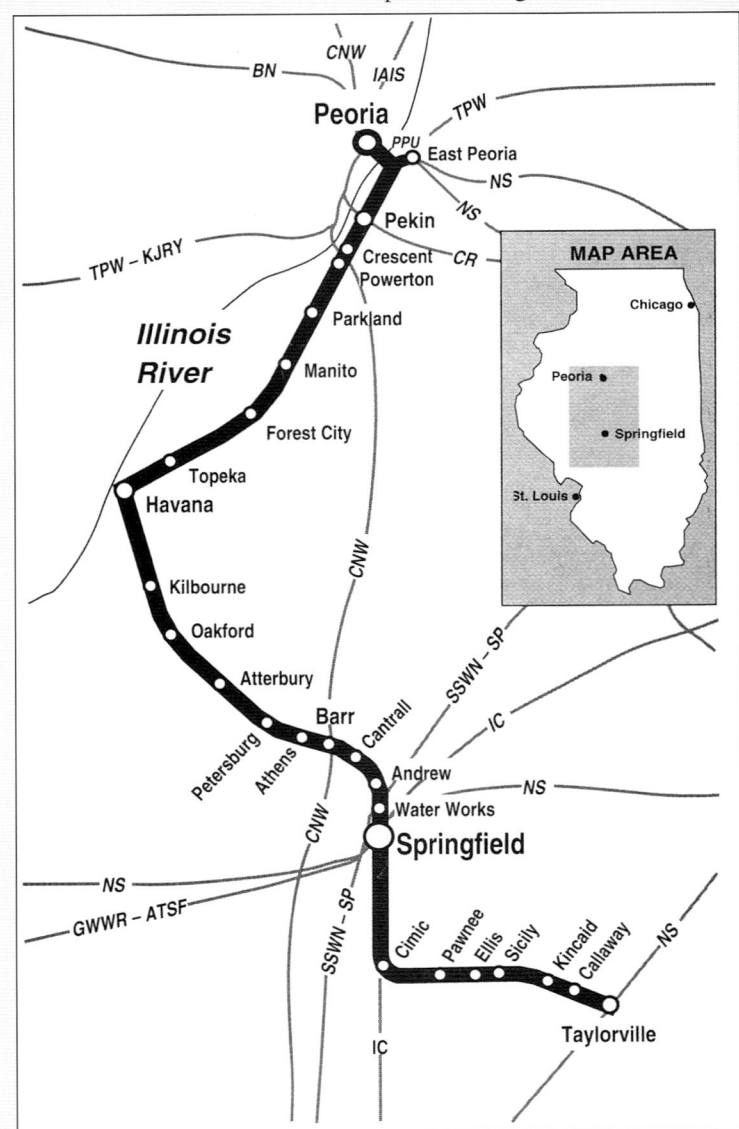

Pawnee and Glenarm via Pawnee Jct., which was later renamed Cimic. The tiny Pawnee railroad actually built slightly less than four miles of track. The village of Glenarm was on the St. Louis and Chicago's main line. Within three years the citizens of Pawnee realized that their new railroad had not adequately solved their transportation problems. Relations with the St. Louis and Chicago were often difficult, and the larger road was not financially strong. To better secure their financial and economic interests, the citizens of Pawnee elected to extend their little road another five miles west to a connection with the Chicago & Alton at Auburn.

As originally constructed, the tiny Pawnee Railroad could never have survived in the age of the automobile. Its passenger traffic evaporated as hard roads expanded through central Illinois. Competition from trucks would steal away most of its agricultural business in later years. Survival for the Pawnee lay hidden under the corn fields that bordered the Pawnee's right of way. Millions of tons of coal extended for miles underground in every direction. A new mine had recently begun operations just outside of Pawnee, and it soon attracted the attention of powerful men in Chicago.

In 1903 a new partnership, the Illinois Midland Coal Company, was forged by Samuel Insul and Francis Peabody to mine and transport coal from central Illinois to the rapidly expanding electric utilities of Chicago. The furnaces of Insul's Chicago Edison and Commonwealth Electric would require up to a half-million tons of coal a year. As they bought up the mineral rights in the area surrounding the Pawnee Railroad's right-of-way, Insul and Peabody realized that control of the Pawnee would facilitate transportation of the coal to Chicago. By mid-1905 the Illinois Midland Coal Company had gained control of the Pawnee Railroad. Plans were almost immediately made to extend the railroad east to Taylorville, where connections could be established with the Baltimore and Ohio and Wabash railroads. The eastward extension of the Pawnee would also facilitate development of the coal deposits along the new right-of-way. Eventually seven Peabody coal mines would line the Pawnee. Half of the coal would go to Chicago area power plants, the other half would be sold on the open market. The extension was completed in 1906 as the Pawnee became the Chicago & Illinois Midland. As the coal began to flow, a new roundhouse and shop facility were constructed in Taylorville. The reconstructed line was slightly over 26 miles in length.

Ever mindful of rising expenses, Commonwealth Edison and Peabody Coal Company officials often discussed proposals to reduce coal transportation costs by barging coal from central Illinois to Chicago on the Illinois River. Early plans envisioned the extension of the C&IM west from the new C&NW connection at Compro (west of Auburn) to the Illinois River. Later plans focused on an extension of the C&IM north to the Illinois River in the vicinity of Havana. Fortunately for the C&IM, at the very time that its leaders were exploring alternatives for expansion, the Chicago, Peoria, and St. Louis was nearing total financial collapse and possible abandonment. President Gilcrest realized that the C&IM could purchase an existing railroad that connected Springfield with Havana and Peoria. The C&IM would gain direct access to the Illinois River at two locations. After complicated negotiations, the C&IM leadership persuaded Commonwealth Edison to purchase the CP&StL. During the negotiations it was also agreed that Commonwealth Edison would cooperate with Middle West Utilities in the construction of a new power plant near Pekin Illinois.

The 1926 extension of the railroad north of Springfield mandated a change in coal train operations. Traffic formerly exchanged at Auburn and Compro was shifted to Ridgely yard in Springfield (Alton) and Barr, near Athens (CNW). Traffic on the Compro exten-

ABOVE - *The Engine Crew Board, November, 1985 at Diesel Shop Springfield.* (Roger Holmes)

sion withered. In 1928 the new power plant at Powerton opened, significantly increasing tonnage on the line to Pekin. Even though most railroads suffered great losses of traffic during the 1930's, the C&IM's business actually increased. In early 1933 coal was rerouted from all rail routes to the newly-opened transfer Dock A at Havana. Success with Dock A led to the construction of a much larger and more efficient Dock B. As the transfer operations gained in efficiency, direct interchange of coal traffic with the Chicago area railroads rapidly decreased. Throughout the Depression the C&IM aggressively sought local business and interchange traffic from connecting railroads. The onset of World War II filled the railroad with record amounts of tonnage.

At the end of 1945 C&IM trains were pulled by a well-maintained fleet of 28 steam engines, including three 4-4-0's, four 0-8-0's, eight 2-8-2's, and thirteen 2-10-2's. Unlike most other railroads, the C&IM continued to add more steam engines to its roster. As older 2-8-2's wore out and parts became more expensive, the C&IM purchased three 0-8-0's and thirteen 2-10-2's from other railroads to supplement its roster. For ten years the C&IM remained faithful to steam power. Coal was plentiful and inexpensive. The Taylorville shop crews were well-versed in locomotive repairs. Gradually the roster evolved as the 4-4-0's and most of the 2-8-2's were retired. By 1950 the 0-8-0's and 2-10-2's dominated the road's operations.

As the roster evolved the C&IM began a slow process of modifying its operations to meet the changing transportation needs of its customers. By mid-1949 the scheduled time freights were discontinued. Apparently the management felt that the merchandise traffic could be moved more efficiently on extra freights. As passenger traffic declined trains #5 & 8 were discontinued. The remaining trains made a Springfield-to-Pekin turn until May of 1953, when #6 & 7 were also discontinued. After 1953 local freights #22 & 23 were the only remaining scheduled trains in the timetable. In 1950 and 1951 Peabody Coal closed Mines #57 and 59 in Springfield. In 1952 Peabody Coal began closing the smaller mines (#7-8-9 and 58) that lined the Taylorville Division. In their place, Peabody constructed Mine #10 at Ellis, Illinois, which began operations in July of 1952. Mine #10 was capable of loading as many as one hundred eighty 70 ton or two hundred sixty 50 ton cars per day. C&IM built a new yard at Ellis to serve the mine. As the smaller mines closed, the number of mine runs was radically reduced from twenty to five per day.

In 1955 the C&IM made the fateful decision to purchase diesel locomotives. The economics of dieselization overwhelmed its loyalty to steam. Amazingly, five EMD SD9's could do the work of ten 2-10-2's on the coal extras and the regular freights. Six EMD SW1200's could replace five 0-8-0's, seven 2-10-2's and two 2-8-2's on the mine runs and switch jobs. Although the operations remained essentially the same, the diesels could haul longer trains more quickly and efficiently.

The steam-era pattern of operations remained in effect until the 1960's, when radical changes in Commonwealth Edison's operations forced the C&IM to restructure its service. During the 1960's Commonwealth Edison built several nuclear power plants, significantly reducing its need for coal. As it closed smaller coal fired plants, Commonwealth Edison decided to use unit trains to transport a large percentage of its coal directly from the mines to the remaining coal fired plants. The transfer of coal to barges at Havana significantly decreased. In 1967, the C&IM suffered its greatest loss of business when Commonwealth Edison finished the new Kincaid power plant directly across the road from Peabody Mine #10. Shipment of coal from Mine #10 was cut in half. Responding to stricter environmental laws, Commonwealth Edison was compelled to reduce its use of sulfur-laden Illinois coal by using coal from Montana and Wyoming. Unit trains from the West began deliveries in 1969. By 1982 the Powerton generating plant stopped burning Illinois coal. Throughout the 1960's and 1970's the political and legal environment continued to change, forcing Commonwealth Edison to re-evaluate its ownership of the C&IM.

Given the situation, the C&IM had to further restructure its operations. In 1964 the C&IM stopped soliciting interline carload traffic. At the same time many of C&IM's local customers stopped using the railroad's services. Although it continued to provide service to commercial customers in Springfield and Pekin, the C&IM stopped running freight trains to the P&PU yard in East Peoria. By 1969 delivery of interline traffic on the north end of the railroad was changed from East Peoria to Pekin, and the C&IM sold its 25% ownership of the P&PU. As the number of trains operated per day significantly decreased, large numbers of employees were laid off.

Then, just at the point when it appeared the railroad might wither for the lack of business, coal trains from the Western states began to arrive. Fortunately, the C&IM had not surrendered its operating rights on the P&PU mainline. In 1969 BN unit trains began running from Peoria to Havana. In addition, from 1971 until 1982 the CNW delivered two Monterey, Illinois-to-Powerton coal trains each day at Barr. Coal tonnage rebounded and remained steady until 1988. Yet even though the railroad was profitable and increasingly efficient, Commonwealth Edison decided that ownership of the railroad was no longer expedient or necessary. Commonwealth Edison would ultimately go through a radical restructuring of its own operations, and in 1987 it sold the C&IM to private investors.

Although relations with Commonwealth Edison remained positive and coal tonnage continued to move to Powerton and Havana, the new management realized that the C&IM had to diversify its traffic base to survive in a rapidly changing economic environment. Since the C&IM still maintained open interchange with eleven railroads, it once again solicited interline traffic. In 1989 The C&IM opened a lumber reload facility at the yard in Springfield. Aggressively seeking traffic for the anemic Taylorville Division, the C&IM signed contracts to move garbage to the newly opened Christian County land fill. Reviving direct interchange with the P&PU at East Peoria, the C&IM initiated a new freight train named the Expediter to carry the interline traffic. The new service began in the spring of 1992.

Unfortunately, as the carload business increased, the coal business collapsed a second time. In 1988 the C&IM handled over 5.5 million tons of coal. By 1991 the total tonnage had dropped to 3.3 million tons. The Powerton generating plant significantly reduced its production to undergo maintenance and upgrading. At the same time Commonwealth Edison significantly reduced the transfer of coal at the Havana facility.

The management team led by George Stern responded quickly. The railroad negotiated significant changes in its labor agreements, cut capital spending, and laid off a large number of employees. Engines were leased to other railroads to raise funds. Planning for a new barge-loading facility at Crystal Lake accelerated. Yet, as they searched for solutions, the team realized that the long-term survival of the C&IM was still based in the movement of coal. And right in their backyard was the Kincaid generating plant that still burned Illinois coal from Mine #10. Given the economic, political, and environmental realities of the 1990's, the C&IM would thrive if it could deliver Western coal to Kincaid. After prolonged negotiations and demonstrations, coal service to Kincaid resumed on November 10, 1994.

After its sale to private investors, the C&IM was independent for eight years. Traffic patterns continued to fluctuate. As the major railroads in the nation consolidated into larger companies, the C&IM lost several of its friendly connections. The Union Pacific acquired the Chicago & North Western and the Southern Pacific. Canadian National purchased the Illinois Central. Kansas City Southern took over the Gateway Western.

The pattern was duplicated in the non-railroad realm, when Cargill purchased the Pillsbury plant in Springfield and Commonwealth Edison sold its coal-fired generating stations. Commonwealth Edison even sold the Havana coal transfer operation. Yet throughout the changes moving coal continued to be the C&IM's principal task. By 1995 the traffic patterns had completely reversed, as most of the coal flowed south to Powerton, Havana, and Kincaid instead of north. The trains were heavier and longer than ever before, and connecting railroads often provided the power. Unlike a host of neighboring railroads that were abandoned or merged into other corporations, the C&IM continued to serve its customers in the center of Illinois. On February 9, 1996, the C&IM was sold to the Genesee and Wyoming company. Renamed the Illinois and Midland, the railroad continues to haul coal and other commodities in the 21st century.

TABLE OF CONTENTS

INTRODUCTION	3
PEORIA TO PEKIN ON THE P&PU MAINLINE	8
PEKIN TO POWERTON	18
POWERTON TO HAVANA	32
HAVANA TO RIDGELY TOWER	44
SPRINGFIELD	58
AVENUE TOWER TO CIMIC VIA THE ILLINOIS CENTRAL	78
CIMIC TO TAYLORVILLE	86
C&IM POWER LEASED TO NEIGHBORING RAILROADS	102
C&IM POWER ROSTER	106
C&IM CABOOSES AND FREIGHT EQUIPMENT	118

LEFT - *Entrance Sign C&IM Yard Springfield, April 24, 1994. (Scott Muskopf)*

C&IM ROSTER INFORMATION
STEAM ENGINES IN 1950

Road Number	Class	Type	Year Built	Notes
500-501	A1	4-4-0	1927	
502	A1	4-4-0	1928	
527	E4	2-8-0	1923	from Minerets & Western
540-541	D2	0-8-0	1937	
545-546	D3	0-8-0	1929	from Manufacturers Ry. in 1944
547-548	D4	0-8-0	1926	from K&IT in 1949
550-551	F4	2-8-2	1928	
552	F4	2-8-2	1931	
560-561	F5	2-8-2	1922/1923	from DL&W in 1945
600-601	G1	2-10-2	1927	
602-603	G2	2-10-2	1929	
651-659	G3	2-10-2	1917	from Wabash 1940-1950
700-703	H1	2-10-2	1931	

STEAM ENGINES ADDED 1951-1953

Road Number	Class	Type	Year Built	Notes
549	D4	0-8-0	1926	from K&IT in 1953
751-754	H2	2-10-2	1925/1926	from ACL 1951
755-759	H2	2-10-2	1925/1926	from ACL 1952

Engines retired 1950: 4-4-0: 501
Engines retired 1951: 2-8-2: 527, 560-561
Engines retired 1952: 2-10-2: 653, 659
Engines retired 1953: 4-4-0: 500, 502. 2-10-2: 651-652, 658
Engines retired 1955: 0-8-0: 540-541, 545-549. 2-8-2: 550-552
2-10-2: 600-603, 654-657, 700-703, 751-759

DIESELS

Road Number	Type	Year Built	Notes
18, 19	SW1200	4/55	Single control, MU equipped.
20-23	SW1200	11/55	Dual control, MU equipped.
30-31	RS1325	9/60	Dual control, MU equipped. Only two built by EMD
50-54	SD9	11/55	Dual control, MU equipped.
60, 61	SD18	12/61, 6/62	Dual control, MU equipped, Low Nose
70-75	SD38-2	5/74	Dual control, MU equipped, Low nose.
80-84	SD20	1959	Single control, MU equipped, Chop nose. Rebuilt from SD24's. Only pre-owned units, purchased from Illinois Central 1/96.

Dispositions:
SW1200 19 sold to Commonwealth Edison 10/79.
SD9 51 retired in 1982. Stored at Shops into the late 1990's.
SD38-2's 70-75 sold to Union Pacific 1-2/95.
Remaining engines conveyed to I&M Railroad in February 1996.

PEORIA TO PEKIN ON THE P&PU MAINLINE

ABOVE - Milepost 0 for the Chicago & Illinois Midland was located at Peoria Union Station on the Peoria & Pekin Union. The C&IM gained access to Peoria in 1926 when it purchased the northern portion of the Chicago, Peoria, and St. Louis. The purchase included a 25% ownership of the P&PU, which operated the Peoria area terminal facilities for its owners. The C&IM provided daily passenger service from Springfield to Peoria from 1926 until August of 1939, when the trains stopped running north of Pekin Illinois. On April 30, 1955, Mikado 550 leads one of ten passenger specials that the Rock Island and C&IM ran for school children from the Chicago area. The children toured historic sites around Springfield. Rock Island provided the commuter coaches and a dining car for the specials.
(John Harrigan, Merlyn Lauber Collection)

ABOVE - C&IM class H2 2-10-2 757 waits near the coaling tower for its crew in the early 1950's. From 1926 until 1955 C&IM's steam engines were turned and serviced at the P&PU's roundhouse located in Peoria on the west side of the Illinois River. C&IM freights terminated in East Peoria yard on the east side of the river. The engines then crossed the river for servicing. During the steam era C&IM engine crews normally rested in Peoria while the P&PU's switch crews prepared their trains for the return trip to Springfield.
(John Harrigan, Merlyn Lauber Collection)

ABOVE - On March 8, 1972 C&IM SD9 51 leads a four-unit set of EMD SD's waiting for the delivery of a BN unit coal train to the P&PU yard at East Peoria. Originally the C&IM received unit coal trains from Wyoming in the yard. Throughout its existence the C&IM received and delivered regular freight via the P&PU facilities. The P&PU delivered C&IM's connecting traffic to the Rock Island, the TP&W, the M&StL, the C&NW, the CB&Q, (BN), the Nickel Plate, (N&W/NS), and the Pennsylvania, (PC/CR). Cars received from these connecting roads were assembled into trains for movement south on the C&IM. *(Railscene by Steve Rippeteau)*

ABOVE - From the spring of 1992 until May of 1995, the Midland operated a weekday-only job from Springfield to East Peoria called the Expediter. A modified union agreement allowed the railroad to use two-person crews for the first time in the railroad's history. However, if the train handled more than thirty-five cars an extra brakeman was added. The Expediter was unique because it was a turn-job that handled connection and through traffic from Springfield to East Peoria, and also switched local customers as needed. Normally, a single road unit handled the Expediter. But on August 23, 1993 four units are necessary because of a healthy cut of wheat from the BN way-billed to Cargill at Springfield. SD9's #54 and 50, spliced by SW1200's #21 and 23, depart P&PU's East Peoria Yard and head south at Wesley. *(Ed Johnson)*

ABOVE - On a fine December 19, 1994, a lone RS1325 handles a four-car Expediter under the signal bridge at Wesley. These signals govern all northbound movements from P&PU's CTC double track into East Peoria Yard and over the Illinois River Bridge. The double track's furthest north cross-over was also located here. Today, the P&PU dispatcher has lined Extra 31 South onto the southbound main, which was the normal routing. Had a coal train been set out at Wesley by BN or CNW, the dispatcher could use the northbound main to keep Extra 31 South rolling without delay. Behind the train are P&PU's Peoria-area TOFC facility and engine house.
(Scott Muskopf)

ABOVE - Gliding past the Illinois Grain elevator north of Hilliards, SD18 60 leads two SD9's and SD18 61 pulling a Wyoming coal train of new BN and C&IM gondolas south to Havana on June 29, 1972. The Extra 60 South will use the P&PU double track mainline from Wesley to Pekin Tower. *(Railscene by Steve Rippeteau)*

ABOVE - In the early 1970's, delivery of western coal trains was relocated to Wesley or to milepost 7 on the P&PU double track. This move eased congestion in both the BN and P&PU yard's in the Peoria area. In June of 1984, the Powerton Switch Job has delivered a BN train to the south bound main at Wesley, while ICG GP38ac 9540 leads train #276 from Mattoon, Illinois toward East Peoria on the northbound main. Engines 75-61-72 are retrieving their caboose, and will head south, either to pick up an inbound BN train at milepost 7 or return to Powerton caboose light. *(John & Roger Kujawa)*

ABOVE - The Powerton Switch Job, with two SD38-2's, leads a loaded BN coal train on the double track near Hilliards, on August 29, 1983. The vantage point is the Shade-Lohmann Bridge carrying the newly constructed I-474 bypass around Peoria across the Illinois River. Lead unit #71 has been freshly repainted while the trailing unit #73 is wearing the original scheme, complete with a herald on the rear of the long hood. In 1983, the Midland handled 399 western coal trains from BN to the Powerton Plant. Big Horn Mine (Kleenburn, Wyoming), originated 201 trains; East Decker Mine (Montana), 104 trains; and West Decker Mine (Montana), 94 trains. These mines also loaded trains for the Havana Coal Transfer Plant.

(Mike Hofe, Roger Bee Collection)

ABOVE - Former Wabash 2-10-2 655 leads an extra south near Grove in the early 1950's. C&IM normally ran an extra carrying regular freight south from Peoria in the late morning and second freight just before midnight. The freights carried cars for delivery to industries in Springfield as well as others for connecting roads on the south end of the railroad. Some of the cars will continue south to make connections with the Wabash at Taylorville. *(John Harrigan, Merlyn Lauber Collection)*

ABOVE - The P&PU mainline skirts the shoreline of Pekin Lake from Grove to Pekin, providing a water-level route for fast train operations. C&IM class H2 2-10-2 756 rolls an extra south along the double track mainline midway between Wesley and Pekin. For many years C&IM second class freight #45 left East Peoria at 11:30AM, with a scheduled arrival at Taylorville at 7:30PM. The schedule allowed two hours for picking up and setting out cars at Springfield. The extra south will closely adhere to the old schedule as it progresses south. *(John Harrigan, Merlyn Lauber Collection)*

ABOVE - Less than a year old, SD9's #54 and 51 bring an extra south into Pekin, Illinois. C&IM purchased five SD9's to replace the sixteen 2-10-2's that were still on the roster in November of 1955. In theory, two SD9's were available to handle the extra freights north of Springfield, while three SD9's were available to run the Quiver Turns and Short Turns hauling coal on the south end of the railroad. The P&PU's main line was protected with automatic block signals from Wesley Jct. to Pekin Tower. Freights were allowed 35 mph while using the P&PU mainline. *(John Harrigan, Merlyn Lauber Collection)*

ABOVE - In the early 1970's SD9 52 leads three other SD9's on a Havana unit coal train down the P&PU mainline north of Pekin. Changing patterns in Commonwealth Edison's coal purchases spurred by stricter federal environmental regulations have shifted the movement of coal on the C&IM. In the past the majority of coal loads were received from mines or connecting roads on the south end of the railroad. Now, more coal loads are received from mines located on other railroads that arrive at the north end of the C&IM. This pattern will continue into the 1990's.
(Railscene by Steve Rippeteau)

ABOVE - The Manito Roadswitcher, with units #74-60-72, handles a BN train for Powerton on February 3, 1991. On September 13, 1990, C&IM began operating Roadswitcher crews out of Manito, replacing the Powerton Roadswitcher. Newly signed union contracts allowed these crews to operate 25 miles in either direction. The railroad was not required to use a fireman. Two crews worked out of this location five days a week, serving the Powerton Generating Station and the Havana Coal Transfer Plant, along with switching and interchange at Pekin. Today's train is rounding a curve near milepost 7, the location of an air shed adjacent to the main line that enabled sitting coal trains to be charged with air while awaiting the arrival of C&IM crews. *(James DuBose)*

ABOVE - On November 18, 1989, the Extra 6:30AM Powerton Job is heading north to get BN train 116DD016, which has been delivered to milepost 7. The BN units have cut off and are in the clear at the North Pekin crossover as the Midland rumbles past. Meets such as this were common on the double track. When C&IM crews delivered an empty train and picked up loads, it was known as a balance swap. Today, the Midland is running engine light, which indicates there is no empty train for the BN crew. The BN will then run engine light back across the river and tie up. The C&IM always used coal train symbols from connecting roads, and this is the 116th train from DD (West Decker, Montana) to 016 (Commonwealth Edison/Powerton Station). *(Ed Johnson)*

14

ABOVE - It's Wednesday, April 5, 1989, and the 9:00AM Powerton Roadswitcher has coal train 36DD016 in tow as it exits the P&PU double track at milepost 8.7. Engineer Charlie Myers has throttled the units down and is preparing for the 10 mph crawl through Pekin. The track diverging to the left is the Ice House Track, which allowed the P&PU to access Pekin industries, their Farm Yard and the former Peoria Terminal (PT) Yard along the Illinois River.
(John & Roger Kujawa)

ABOVE - On April 9, 1968 C&IM SW1200 23 is assigned to the 10AM Pekin yard job. The Pekin job is passing Pekin tower, which controlled Illinois Central's and C&IM's access to the south end of the P&PU mainline. The C&IM interchanged with the Santa Fe Pekin branch and the New York Central's Peoria and Eastern line at Pekin tower. Cars for interchange were left on designated tracks a few hundred feet east of the tower. *(Ed Johnson)*

15

ABOVE - SD38-2's 71 and 73 ease into Pekin with Powerton loads as they negotiate a tight curve and the crossing of the Peoria & Eastern at Pekin Tower on September 17, 1983. The Peoria & Eastern (NYC) main line from Indianapolis to Pekin met the P&PU at Pekin Tower. The P&E main crossed the P&PU and extended south to the Whiskey Main located along the Illinois River. Pekin Tower also marked the end of Santa Fe's Ancona, Illinois to Pekin branch. The Midland maintained friendly connections with the P&E and Santa Fe, exchanging traffic here until the early 1980's. *(Ed Johnson)*

ABOVE - C&IM's 7:00AM Powerton Job is bullying its way down 3rd St. in Pekin, on March 14, 1986. Engines 74-61-75 are heading north to get a BN coal train at milepost 7. This is one of three places where C&IM trains ran on street trackage. The others were Havana (until 1949) and Madison Street in Springfield (until 1937). C&IM Stations and Special Instructions #6 state: *"between Susannah and Second St. crossing, all trains 10 mph."*

(Trey Kunz)

16

ABOVE - Running north on 3rd Street are SD9's 53,54, and 51 pulling an empty BN coal train. In two blocks they will pass Pekin Tower. The Powerton based crew will take the empties to the P&PU for delivery to the BN in Peoria. In the late 1970's the SD38-2's were primarily used on the BN and CNW repaying horsepower hours, necessitating the use of the older engines. *(Railscene by Steve Rippeteau)*

BELOW - The C&IM and the IC accessed Pekin Tower by running down 3rd Street in Pekin. As the trains moved south they encountered a sharp curve before heading into the street. In October of 1974 SD38-2 70 leads SD18 61 and SD38-2's 73/72 with a low sulphur coal train for Havana received from the BN. The train will follow 3rd street south for another three blocks to the junction where the C&IM and the IC diverge into their respective mainlines. *(Railscene by Steve Rippeteau)*

PEKIN TO POWERTON

ABOVE - Pulling past the Pekin depot, the morning switch crew is preparing to deliver a cut of coal received from the IC to the Standard Brands factory on the south side of town. The Pekin yard job switched 16 industries from milepost 9.23 at Pekin through Crescent to the south yard limits at Powerton, which included the Commonwealth Edison power plant. The Pekin job was normally assigned a 2-8-2, although a 2-10-2 was used to spot the coal trains at the power plant. Lima built class K4 2-8-2 550 frequently drew the Pekin assignment. Hiding behind the 550 is train #7 with engine 502, which will leave Pekin at 3:30PM. *(Robert F. Collins, Morning Sun Books Collection)*

ABOVE - The Powerton Job, with SD38-2's 71-70-72, regains home rails at Pekin on June 1, 1988. The train is rolling by the Pekin depot, which was the northern-most open agency on the Midland until 1972. At that time the Powerton depot became the north-end station and handled all clerical duties. During the summer of 1988, 3rd St. was rebuilt and relocated, eliminating street running for C&IM and IC trains north of the depot. *(Ed Johnson)*

ABOVE - H2 class 2-10-2 758 pulls an extra north past the Pekin depot. A typical extra north would approximately follow train #44's old schedule, leaving Springfield at six in the morning and arriving at Pekin about 8:30AM. Upon arrival in Pekin the extra north would set out high cars (regular freight) for local delivery on the Back Hay track. It would then pull up to the IC River Track crossing and call Pekin Tower for instructions. When Pekin Tower gave permission, the extra north would then pull through town to the 3rd Street trackage and enter the P&PU mainline.
(John Harrigan, Merlyn Lauber Collection)

ABOVE - The 10AM Pekin yard job is pulling loads from Barney Kahn steel which was located just north of the Pekin depot, on October 18, 1971. Next to SW1200 19 is the Pekin engine shed. The engine facility at Pekin was abandoned after the Powerton Yard was expanded and a new diesel servicing facility was built in 1972. The C&IM purchased six SW1200's in 1955 to replace five 0-8-0's and three 2-8-2's. The SW1200's were used on mine runs, yard jobs, and locals. Since there were only five SD9's, one or two SW1200's frequently assisted the SD9's in coal and freight service. *(Ed Johnson)*

19

ABOVE - On September 8, 1983, the 7:00AM Powerton Switch Job rolls an empty train north by the Pekin Warehousing Company, which was used to store whiskey. Legend has it that cooperative conductors of the Pekin yard job were often rewarded with gifts of whiskey from the warehouse dock loaders. Today's Powerton job has only two units. In December 1982, after run-through agreements ended with the CNW and the BN, the C&IM management tried to use only two newer SD's on the Powerton Job. Two locomotives were adequate to handle the tonnage, yet train-braking became an issue when spotting heavy coal trains into the Powerton Plant. By late 1983 operating personnel persuaded management to utilize three SD's to improve the safe handling of the trains in the plant. *(Mike Hofe, Roger Bee Collection)*

ABOVE - On August 28, 1984, Powerton-bound coal with three SD38-2's rolls past the smash-board guarding the former Illinois Central River Track crossing in Pekin. The River Track was IC's connection from their yard in Pekin to industries located along the Illinois River. Rule 13(c) in the C&IM Stations and Special Instructions #5 states: *"A crossing gate is located at Illinois Central Gulf Crossing, Pekin. The normal position of this gate is for C&IM trains. If the gate is against the route to be used trains and engines must be governed by rule 98 (a)."* Much to the dismay of C&IM engineers, the crossing gate was set against them all too often, and sometimes with little time to react. *(Ed Johnson)*

ABOVE - At 12:20pm on July 22, 1971 the Pekin yard crew is switching the Standard Brands factory at Crescent with RS1325 30. Standard Brands produced yeast and syrup at this location. Employees who worked in the days of steam say that Standard Brands often purchased molasses from Cuba. The molasses was loaded into blocks of tank cars at Gulf Coast ports and delivered to the C&IM by the Wabash at Taylorville. An extra north would then bring the molasses to Pekin for delivery by the yard crew. The yard crew also switched the Quaker Oats paper plant, which was located north of the Standard Brands plant. *(Ed Johnson)*

ABOVE - SD38-2's 70, 74 and 73 blast through Crescent with a BBHVC coal train bound for the Havana Coal Transfer Plant on December 14, 1985. The BBHVC (Black Butte to Havana Coal) originated at Black Butte Mine located on the Union Pacific near Point of Rocks, Wyoming. To the left is Pekin Energy Company, formerly Corn Products, and to the right beyond the grade crossing was the former location of C&IM's Pekin Yard. In the far background next to the train are gray covered hoppers sitting on the Back Hay Track. This track was used by the Extras North and South to exchange "high" cars with the Pekin Switch Job until 1972, when the exchange of local cars was relocated to the newly expanded Powerton Yard.

(John & Roger Kujawa)

LEFT - Train #6 with 4-4-0 502 rolls under the C&NW Nelson-Benld main line at Crescent in the early 1950's. The train includes a 30' RPO baggage and a coach. It is due at Pekin shortly after nine. After unloading the mail, express, and passengers, the crew will back the train to Crescent and turn the train on the wye. Then they will service the engine. Later in the morning the train will return to Pekin to await the mid-afternoon departure of #7. *(Railscene by David Lewis)*

ABOVE - In mid-1952 the morning Pekin crew pulls a cut of IC hoppers through Crescent for delivery to the Commonwealth Edison Powerton generating station, which is just on the other side of the C&NW mainline. The coal was delivered from mines in southern Illinois by the IC to Pekin. The delivery was an interesting move as the C&IM and IC mainlines paralleled one another through town. Large coal trains from the IC had to be pulled north onto the P&PU main and then reversed for transfer to the C&IM. Behind G2 class 2-10-2 603 are the C&IM's Crescent engine facilities and wye. Passenger engines and freight engines from coal extras that brought trains to Powerton were turned and serviced here. *(Joe Collias)*

ABOVE - On November 8, 1995, the Powerton Roadswitcher, with RS1325 30 and SD9 50, spots tank cars at the recently constructed rail-to-barge facility on Crystal Lake, south of Pekin. The C&IM acquired this 46 acre parcel of land from the city of Pekin in 1993. Crystal Lake provided the northern most still-water port on the Illinois River that was open year-round. To serve the new facility, the Midland constructed a loop track by extending the Crescent Wye and swinging it around the property to re-connect with the mainline. The loop ran through a relocated Mississippi River bridge that was used to trans-load grain, alcohol, distiller's grains and by-products shipped from Pekin Energy and Midwest Grain Products to Gulf-Coast markets. The CNW quickly took advantage of the new facility, diverting several grain trains from East St. Louis to Crescent for trans-loading. The Midland handled about 3,000 loads of grain at this facility in 1995. The loop also re-established an important connection with Pekin Paperboard. *(Gary Helling)*

ABOVE - The lifeblood of the modern C&IM was Commonwealth Edison's massive Powerton Generating Station, shown here on November 28, 1999. Built in early 1928 by the Super Power Company of Illinois, it was originally jointly owned by several utility companies. By December 1, 1930, three generating units were operating. Com Ed expanded the plant in 1972 by adding generating unit #5, and again in 1975 with unit #6, which were the largest coal-fired generating units in Commonwealth Edison's history. The expansion included a unit train rotary car dumper. By 1995 the Powerton Station was consuming 14,000 tons of coal per day, with a rated production capacity of nearly 1.8 million megawatts of electricity. *(Ryan Crawford)*

ABOVE - By WWII the Powerton plant was consuming up to 1½ million tons of coal per year. Coal came from several Peabody mines, including mines along the Illinois Central and New York Central, as well as the C&IM. Pekin yard crews typically used 2-10-2's to spot the coal in the plant. G2 class 2-10-2 602 is typical of the engines used on these assignments. Movement of coal into the plant without radios across busy Manito Road was a challenge, especially at night. The engineer had to quickly respond to hand signals from the brakemen who relayed instructions as the cars entered the plant.

(Joe Collias, Richard Wallin Collection)

BELOW - Engine 602 is pulling into track B-1 in Powerton yard with a block of coal from the IC. When the tail end of the train clears Manito Road, the crew will begin the process of spotting the coal into the power plant. Another block of coal from the Taylorville area mines rests on track B-4, also waiting to be spotted in the plant.
(Joe Collias, Richard Wallin Collection)

ABOVE - Class H2 engine 753 coasts down the main at Powerton nearing the south end of the Pekin area yard limits. The Extra South picked up Pekin industry cars from the south end of the Back Hay Track, located a mile north of Powerton. It did not normally pick up cars at Powerton. Normal running time for an extra south from Pekin to Springfield was about four hours. Engine 753 was originally Atlantic Coast Line engine 2013, which C&IM acquired in 1951. *(John Harrigan, Merlyn Lauber Collection)*

ABOVE - The engineer of Extra 70 South picks up orders on the fly as he drags a BN coal train past the two year old Powerton depot in October of 1974. The assignment of four SD's indicates that the train is an Extra South delivering coal to Havana for transfer to barges on the Illinois River. Crews for the Havana trains were drawn from the Springfield Chain Gang, a pool of crews which were assigned to trains on a "first in, first out" basis. The term "chain gang" (in this sense) originated from the permanent assignment of engine crews that worked together using specific locomotives for long periods of time. In a sense they were "chained" to the locomotive. Both Springfield and Taylorville had Chain Gangs crews.

(Railscene by Steve Rippeteau)

ABOVE - On February 20, 1995, SD18 60 and SW1200 20 share the track leading into the Powerton engine shed. Built during the Powerton Yard expansion in 1972, this was C&IM's newest engine shed. The Powerton shed is unique because it has a flat roof, whereas the older engine houses at Pekin, Havana and Taylorville had steeply pitched roofs. Locomotives were serviced using an air-operated sand bin at the Powerton shed. C&IM's engine sheds were built to accommodate an SW1200. In the shed today is ex-BN, now NREX SW1200 232, which American Milling leased to switch the Crystal Lake transload facility. *(Paul Fries)*

ABOVE - Run-through power in the modern era was no stranger to C&IM. A run-through agreement with Burlington Northern commenced September 15, 1978 and lasted until December 1982. This pool power arrangement eliminated the need for balance swaps on the double track. During this time period it was common to see nothing but foreign power hauling Midland coal trains, while C&IM's SD38-2's, SD18's, and SD9's were used to pay back horse power hours. BN SD40-2's 7047 and 7821 are spliced by U30C 5379, as the morning Powerton Switch Job brings a coal train into the yard. The train will duck under the Manito Road overpass and diverge into the B Yard. After the train is yarded, it will be shoved into the plant by a C&IM switcher in three cuts. *(John & Roger Kujawa)*

ABOVE - In 1980 a run-through coal train with CNW SD45 901, UP U30C 2891, UP C30-7 2444 and UP SD40 3045, heads into A-1 track at Powerton with a coal train for Havana. When the Powerton plant was expanded in 1975, two tracks were built to accommodate 110-car western coal trains. Designated A-1 and A-2, each track held 127 cars. The north end of A-2 track was also known as the pit, where locomotives laid over while coal trains were emptied. The pit was a fueling station which included immersion heater hook-ups for shut-down locomotives. The CNW mainline from Nelson to Madison crosses the C&IM in the background. On January 10, 1993, the Crescent connection with the CNW was completed at this location, allowing the CNW to deliver coal directly to the Midland, by-passing the P&PU double track. Delivery of Powder River Basin coal trains was initiated at the same time the connection was opened. *(John & Roger Kujawa)*

ABOVE - The Powerton Yard is at capacity on a September day in 1983. The morning switch job is pulling empties from the plant, while several cabooses await their next assignment. BN caboose 10254 was being pulled from the empty train and was set out on the Commonwealth Edison Ash track, which the railroad used as a caboose track. BN caboose 12228 and C&IM caboose 76 sit patiently on A-2, coupled to an empty coal train that was recently unloaded. Cabooses were used in pool service long after the locomotive run through agreements ended. CNW/UP cabooses were used until 1987, while BN cabooses could be found on C&IM coal trains into the early 1990's. C&IM caboose 76 was the last caboose ever purchased by the Midland.
(John & Roger Kujawa)

LEFT - It's Sunday, September 17, 1989, and the Extra 1:15PM Powerton Roadswitcher leads the 86DD016 coal loads by the Powerton depot. Running long hood first, engineer Kathy Guy is utilizing engine 75's dual cab controls. In the depot's bay window clerk Karen Stauthammer is carefully recording all 110 car numbers on her switch list. Before computers arrived in December 1989, handwritten switch lists and way bills were the norm. Today's engine consist, 75-60-70, is rather unusual in that all the units are facing north. The normal arrangement of three road units on the Midland was two engines facing north and one facing south. This made the modification of locomotive consists at Springfield more efficient, allowing a hostler to remove the north unit on days when only two units were needed. *(Hal Collins)*

LEFT - The Manito Road Switcher spots a BN train inside the Powerton Station on August 31, 1991. By the early 1980's, road units had supplanted switchers for spotting the coal. Switch crews had a special responsibility while placing coal to the Plant. They had to be absolutely certain that the rotary coupler ends were properly aligned. If not, the drawbars of the coal hoppers would be twisted like tin foil! Inside the plant there were three tracks on which to spot coal: #9, #10, and #11. Together these tracks held 124, 100-ton coal hoppers or gondolas, providing more than sufficient capacity for Powerton trains that religiously ran with 110 cars. The ladder and platform to the left is a brakeman stand. In the days before radio communication the brakeman stood on the platform to relay signals between the engineer and the other brakemen spotting and uncoupling the cars inside the plant. *(Scott Muskopf)*

BELOW - On May 19, 1985, the 4:00PM Powerton Yard Job is preparing to spot coal. The train is heading down B-1 track, which allowed trains leaving the mainline to access the power plant lead. Once the caboose clears the crossover from the main to the B Yard, the conductor will throw the switch and the train will reverse direction. The caboose will be "kicked" to the Ash track, and spotting will commence. The B Yard was comprised of five tracks: B-1 through B-4 and a rip track, which together could hold 370 100-ton coal cars. The power today is SD38-2's 72 and 71 spliced by SD18 61. In the 1980's and early 1990's this was a common engine consist for the Powerton Job. The railroad felt that newer and older power could be mixed at Powerton because of the short shuttling of coal trains. This freed up newer SD38-2's, used in three unit sets, for the longer Havana and Springfield to Pekin runs. *(Gary Powell, Ryan Crawford Collection)*

LEFT - Train #6 skirts Powerton yard as it nears completion of its run from Springfield. The three A1 class 4-4-0's were built in 1927/28 for the expanded C&IM. Normally two A1's were needed to power the Springfield to Peoria passenger trains. The third engine was held in reserve or used on extra's. Passenger service between Taylorville and Auburn on the south end of the railroad was discontinued in 1932. The C&IM did not provide scheduled passenger service between Cimic and Springfield during the five-year time period when passenger trains ran on both the north and south ends of the railroad.
(Joe Collias, Richard Wallin Collection)

ABOVE - New Year's Day 1983 finds SD18's 61 and 60 sandwiching SD9 50, as the Powerton Job sets an empty train over to the A Yard. Powerton crews normally handled the local switching from Powerton to Pekin. They also picked up and delivered Powerton coal trains from the P&PU double track. Springfield-based Chain Gang crews normally handled the Havana coal trains from the double track. When necessary the Powerton crews could pick up Havana trains and bring them to the A Yard to keep the P&PU double track fluid. A Chain Gang crew would then pick up the Havana train later in the day. *(Mark Lynn, Roger Bee Collection)*

BELOW - SW1200 18, SD18 60 and SD9 54 team up to switch out bad order cars from a previously-emptied Com Ed coal train in the A Yard. The A Yard was a holding point for Powerton coal empties. C&IM carmen inspected empty trains and set up the air in the A Yard before the Powerton Job returned the trains to the BN. Normal routine called for switching out the bad orders and setting them over to the south end of the B Yard for the Extra South to handle to Shops. The C&IM supplemented its income by repairing bad-order foreign cars at Shops. Very few of these new red and black CWEX Bethgons will be set out today. The A Yard was renamed Crescent Yard on January 10, 1993 when CNW began using the new Crescent connection.
(Steve Smedley, Ryan Crawford Collection)

ABOVE and LEFT - Hauling a long string of 70 ton coal gondolas loaded at Mine #10, extra 51 north arrives at the south end of Powerton yard. The second half of the train consists of empty BN hoppers picked up at Havana. The extra crew will set out the loads in the B Yard and then place the empty hoppers on Stoehrs siding for later delivery to the BN via the P&PU. Caboose 65 trails the long consist as it enters the yard. Note that Powerton yard is being expanded to handle an increase in tonnage. Commonwealth Edison was in the midst of a significant expansion of the Powerton generating station. June 9, 1971

(Railscene by Steve Rippeteau)

BELOW - Having completed its work after arrival at Powerton, the Extra North crew rearranged their engine consist, setting out SD9 51 and placing the SW1200 in back of the other SD9's. The crew then began to assemble their southbound train, placing the "high cars" from Pekin on the head end and the empty coal gons on the rear. The Havana empties stand behind the southbound train. June 9, 1971

(Railscene by Steve Rippeteau)

31

POWERTON TO HAVANA

ABOVE - The fields are ready for planting at Parkland as Extra 74 South shuttles an empty train from Powerton to Barr on April 3, 1976. The C&IM received coal from the CNW at Barr in the early 1970's for delivery to Commonwealth Edison at Powerton. These trains typically used C&IM or Commonwealth Edison 100-ton gondolas to deliver the coal. The North Western delivered two 60 car coal trains to the C&IM at Barr every day. The trains were loaded at Monterey Mine #1 just south of Carlinville Illinois. Whenever possible, the Monterey coal trains were assigned four SD's to provide enough power to run up Petersburg Hill without doubling the train. *(Ed Johnson)*

ABOVE - Passenger Extra 550 South showers Manito Illinois with cinders as it speeds its load of children to the historic Lincoln sites at New Salem and Springfield. The employee timetable set the speed limit for C&IM's 2-8-2's at 60 mph. Rock Island provided a baggage car, 8 commuter coaches, and a dining car for the trip. A C&IM coach brings up the rear. April 1955. *(John Harrigan, Merlyn Lauber Collection)*

ABOVE - The Manito depot shakes and shudders as the Manito Roadswitcher, with SD38-2's 73-71-72, lugs a BBHVC coal train up the .88% grade at milepost 22 on April 5, 1991. This was the stiffest southbound grade between Pekin and Havana. Today, the engineer is pinching the train air down to comply with Manito's 30 mph speed restriction through town. Between 1984 and December 31, 1992 most of the coal for Havana originated at Black Butte Mine on the UP, although supplemented by BN coal from southern Montana. Occasionally coal trains were *diverted* from other Commonwealth Edison Plants. For example, UP/CNW coal trains could be diverted from Waukegan, Illinois to the dumper at Havana. *(Scott Muskopf)*

BELOW - The Manito Depot sits quietly on July 24, 1999. Depots like this were common in the small towns the C&IM served. This depot sits exactly 22 miles from Peoria Union Station, and handled many a passenger who journeyed to Pekin or Springfield until the demise of passenger service. Mr. Lonnie Boker was the last operator/agent at the Manito depot. Behind the photographer is the Manito annunciator, which gave the "Manito" Morse code signal over the railroad air-waves to alert the Powerton switch crews and the dispatcher as to the whereabouts of trains between Havana and Powerton. *(Ryan Crawford)*

ABOVE - In August 1990, the Midland constructed this new depot on the south side of Manito, which became the operations hub for the Manito Roadswitcher. The building was 12 x 20 feet and had a bathroom, a couple of lockers and phone/fax machine. To the right, 72-71-73 are spotted on the Granger Elevator Track, where the units were kept when not in use. This spur also had immersion heater plug-ins to heat idle locomotives. One mile to the south was the 109-car Union siding, where the Extra North from Springfield exchanged trains with the Manito Roadswitcher. The date is March 24, 1991. In eight months coal traffic to Havana will decrease, and the Roadswitcher will be relocated back to Powerton. *(Scott Muskopf)*

ABOVE - Approaching Forest City, Extra 757 South has plenty of power to roll the train of high cars through town. The H2 class 750's were permitted 60 mph on tangent track, although freights were required to slow to 25mph while passing the coal dock at Forest City. The mixture of cars on this train is typical of C&IM's merchandise extras during the 1950's, with the majority of the cars being boxcars.
(John Harrigan, Melryn Lauber Collection)

ABOVE - Another merchandise extra approaches Forest City on the immaculately maintained C&IM mainline, pulled by former Atlantic Coast Line 2-10-2 751. There is a gentle .24% grade in the four miles between Manito and Forest City that will barely tax the capacity of the 751. The mainline runs straight as an arrow from milepost 15 to the north edge of Forest City at milepost 27. The day is cool and clear, and the engine is running fast.

(John Harrigan, Merlyn Lauber Collection)

BELOW - It is June 11, 1988, and the depot at Forest City still looks tidy even though it hasn't had an operator in quite a while. Replacing a wooden structure at the same location in 1950, its footprint is rather small at 33'x12', and stands 12' tall. Oakford, Manito and Forest City's handsome depots were dimensionally the same, and were decked out with diamond logos and sign boards. Between 1955 and 1964 the Forest City and Manito depots were jointly operated by veteran agent/operator John Crum. *(Don Woodworth)*

ABOVE - RS1325 31 and SD9 50 lead an Expediter southbound through Forest City on December 19, 1994. 31's exhaust is an indication that engineer Charlie McQuern has just notched the throttle out for a little more speed. The tank cars are filled with corn alcohol from Pekin Energy Co. which will be forwarded to Shops for interchange with Southern Pacific. Rickett Grain Company's 1 million bushel elevator looms in the background. In November 1994, Rickett Grain shipped six cars of wheat to the Cargill Plant at Springfield, the first time they utilized C&IM service in 20 years. *(Scott Muskopf)*

ABOVE - A single SD18 heads up the Expediter as it rolls through Topeka on February 20, 1995. Behind the engine is the former location of the Topeka Depot which was manned until 1955. Agent/operator John Crum worked the depot from 1953 to 1955, and lived a mere block from this location. The covered hoppers carried popcorn from Weaver Popcorn in Forest City for interchange to the Norfolk Southern at Springfield. The popcorn will be forwarded by the NS to Weaver's processing plant in Van Buren, Indiana. *(Paul Fries)*

LEFT - RS1325 30 splices SD18's 60 and 61 as they pull an Extra North past Quiver Yard at Havana on January 26, 1971. Normally the coal on this train would originate at Peabody Mine #10 on the Taylorville Division. The train is almost entirely made up of C&IM 70-ton coal gons that the road has been using since 1931. A lone tank car accompanies the coal loads. The C&IM stopped soliciting through traffic from connecting roads in 1964 as Commonwealth Edison began to rethink the role the railroad played in the transportation of coal. In 1965 Com Ed began transporting coal in unit trains directly from the mines to the power plants. In the next few years the C&IM's traffic patterns will significantly change. There will come a time when very few carloads of any type will move between Springfield and Havana. *(Railscene by Steve Rippeteau)*

LEFT - The northbound Expediter, with RS1325 31 and SW1200 23, has just cleared the Havana yard limit board and sails past the former Cimco Farm property on December 19, 1994. The train has a solid block of empty tank cars headed back to Pekin Energy. The tank cars will be loaded with distiller slops and corn alcohol. SW1200 23 will be set out at Powerton Yard to be used at Pekin industries by the Powerton Roadswitcher. The Cimco Farm was established in 1928 as a test bed for crop rotation and animal husbandry to help area farmers. C&IM's Assistant Treasurer, Trevor L. Jones oversaw the daily operations of Cimco Farm until it was closed on December 31, 1953. A spur located on the Cimco property was used only for entertainment purposes when the big-wigs were in town. *(Scott Muskopf)*

ABOVE - All is quiet at Havana Yard (Quiver Yard) on January 12, 1993. Remote control unit SD9 52 occupies the engine house. Behind the engine house is the D Yard, or "Dog Yard," which was built to stage loaded coal trains until they could be dumped. In its most modern form the D Yard could hold five hundred seventy-five 100-ton coal cars. During difficult times in the early 1990's the Midland made good use of its extra yard capacity, storing Itel Leasing covered hoppers in the D Yard. In the foreground C&IM 2002, one of C&IM's home-built sand cars, sits adjacent to the sanding and fueling facilities. Built in May 1960 to accommodate three-unit diesel consists of the Quiver Turns, the facilities also serviced the Havana yard engine. C&IM stopped servicing engines here in September of 1987. To the right is the yard office, opened on July 15, 1962, which contained offices for clerical staff, and a shower/locker room for crewmen. John Crum was agent/operator here from 1964 until the agency closed on December 1, 1989. *(Don Woodworth)*

RIGHT - On June 24, 1979, an Atlas car pusher is placing a BN coal load over the mule pit at Dock C. The mule was the contraption that rose up from between the rails, clasped the coupler, and shoved the car into the dumper. There were two car pushers located along the load tracks, C-1 and C-2. Running on narrow rails, they were powered by electricity located between the tracks. The operator would position himself behind the car, release a steel arm, and shove the load to the mule pit. The man in the picture closed the knuckles on each car so the next load could bump the empty car out of the dumper. The C&IM, in its attempt to make Havana more efficient, replaced Atlas pushers with remote-controlled SD9's in 1991.
(Mike Wise, Ryan Crawford Collection)

LEFT - On April 16, 1996, SD9 52 (fitted with remote control in 1992) pushes a trainload of modern aluminum hoppers toward the dumper. By using a locomotive the railroad minimized possible damage to the cars and allowed the combination of jobs, making the operation more efficient. The tracks on the right are the load tracks C-1 and C-2 where the train crews spotted the coal loads for dumping. The empty tracks, C-3 and C-4 are on the left. As empties rolled off the kick-back track, they passed through the retarder into the empty tracks at a steady four mph. *(Hal Collins)*

RIGHT - Once a load was placed here by an Atlas pusher or remote-controlled SD9, the mule rose up and shoved the car into the dumping shed. When the loaded car entered the shed it would bump the previously unloaded car down the kick-back track. Every 90 seconds a car would be unloaded, and it took about four hours to dump 110 cars. In theory, two unit trains could be dumped per shift. The coal would be sent directly into awaiting barges, or be stockpiled in the coal storage area known as the "football field." The football field derived its name from its similarity to a miniature athletic stadium. The C&IM employed all of the coal dock operators, deck hands, mechanics and laborers and even had its own tug boat "Quiver." The Coal Dock is still in operation as of 2008.
(C&IM Ry., C&IM Chapter NRHS Collection)

LEFT - C&IM 31 switches hopper cars in the yard at Havana in September of 1968. The morning Havana yard crew normally went on duty at 9:10AM. Coal for transloading will be spotted on tracks C-1 and C-2. Then the empties will be pulled. They will also work six or seven local industries. Their work assignments were significantly altered in 1965 as Commonwealth Edison shifted its coal delivery to unit trains. Until December 1986 there were two assigned yard jobs at Havana. *(Terry Cook)*

ABOVE - C&IM 2-10-2 751 pulls a Quiver turn out of the siding at Havana. Automatic block signals will protect the train's movement from Havana to WR tower in Springfield. In the next mile the train will pass the Havana depot and then cross the Illinois Central Champaign to Havana branch. Quiver Turns originated in Taylorville, picking up coal from the mines along the line to Cimic. Entering the IC St. Louis mainline at Cimic, the coal trains ran through Springfield. North of Springfield the Turn could pick up additional loads until it had reached the tonnage limit of the 2-10-2. A typical Quiver turn would move 50 to 60 loads to Havana, returning with a similar train of empty hoppers after the crew had taken time to eat. *(John Harrigan, Merlyn Lauber Collection)*

BELOW - Another Quiver Turn heads south on the mainline at Havana. On a typical day the C&IM would run four to five Quiver turns. Today's train includes a large block of empty IC hoppers. Coal from mines on the Illinois Central was delivered to the C&IM at Pekin, Havana, Springfield, or Cimic, depending upon the location of the mine in southern Illinois. Occasionally the C&IM would "borrow" whole blocks of empty IC hoppers for coal loading when the C&IM ran short of its own cars. Trains of empty hoppers typically would weigh about 1700 tons. Engine 758 will have little difficulty with such a light train as it returns to Taylorville. *(Joe Collias)*

ABOVE - Passenger train #6 pauses at Havana on May 2, 1953 as postal workers unload the mail. The Havana depot was opened in 1949 when the C&IM completed a bypass around the town to avoid three miles of slow trackage/street running closer to the Illinois River. Ironically, the C&IM discontinued trains #5 & #8 shortly after the new depot opened, leaving trains #6 & #7 to handle the remainder of Havana's business. After passenger service was discontinued, the Havana depot continued to house yard clerks and an agent/operator. Later, all operations were moved to the depot adjacent to the Havana yard. The last agent/operator at this depot was Gus Leadman.

(James Shuman)

ABOVE - The northbound Expediter, running engine light, cruises by the Havana Depot en route to East Peoria on August 19, 1994. Engine 30 departed Shops with two SD9's and one SW1200 along with a few cars destined for Pekin and East Peoria. However, because of a computer switch list error, the dispatcher advised the Expeditor crew to leave the entire train, except unit 30, at Kelsey siding. Kelsey was a 76-car siding located about five miles south of Havana Yard. The 30 then ran light engine to East Peoria.

(Ryan Crawford)

ABOVE - Class F4 2-8-2 552 pulls a long cut of empties south from Havana in the mid-1950's. Normally the 2-8-2's would handle local freights 22 and 23, which worked the grain elevators, lumber and coal yards, and team tracks between Springfield and Pekin. Train 23 was scheduled to leave Pekin at 9AM, arriving at Quiver Yard at 10:35AM. After working the yard and taking lunch, the crew would continue south in the early afternoon, with arrival in Springfield about three hours later. Trains #22/23 remained in the schedule until 1956, when the arrival of the SD9's and SW1200's made a significant revision of train operations possible.
(John Harrigan, Merlyn Lauber Collection)

LEFT - A northbound Quiver turn arrives at Havana Junction, pulling past signal 409, which governed the movement of trains over the Illinois Central Havana branch. Quiver Turns typically took eleven hours to complete their work in an age when federal law permitted crews to work 16 hours. H2 class 2-10-2 754 was originally Atlantic Line engine 2013, which the C&IM acquired in 1951. The train is coasting down a slight grade that is almost imperceptible because of the curve. *(Robert F. Collins, Morning Sun Books Collection)*

HAVANA TO RIDGELY TOWER

LEFT - Engine 757 accelerates an extra toward Oakford on a clear fall day in the 1950's. The train is negotiating a mile of tangent track south of Kilbourne that leads to three gentle curves north of Oakford. On a typical day in the mid-1950's the C&IM needed 16 2-10-2's to move its trains. Each 2-10-2 would make one round trip a day. By mid-1953 there were 22 2-10-2's available for service, with six engines either being serviced in the shops or held in reserve.
(Merlyn Lauber Collection)

ABOVE - G2 class 2-10-2 603 pulls a Havana bound Quiver Turn loaded with coal just south of Kilbourne in the mid-1950's. Many C&IM engineers considered the 600's to be the best engines on the railroad. Constructed for the expanded C&IM in 1929, the 603 was equally at home on mine runs and coal trains. Built with 58" drivers and a moderate engine weight of 357,000 pounds, the 603 was limited to 45mph in mainline service. Today's train includes a block of GM&O hoppers delivered at Ridgely Yard on the north end of Springfield. *(Joe Collias)*

BELOW - There is no designated speed restriction on the Pecan Run bridge as extra 753 hustles the merchandise south toward Springfield. A typical freight carried a myriad of commodities for businesses around Springfield and for connecting trains to points south and west. The extra's frequently carried perishables received from the Santa Fe at Pekin for delivery to food wholesalers such as Bunn Capitol Grocery or Mid States Wholesale Grocery in Springfield.
(Joe Collias, Richard Wallin Collection)

ABOVE - The C&IM crosses the Sangamon River three times in the 44 miles between Havana and Springfield. A Quiver Turn powered by 2-10-2 758 will slow to 45 mph as it enters the Sangamon River bridge at milepost 54. Clearing the bridge, engine 758 will ascend a three mile long grade out of the river valley that varies from .53% to 1.04%. Fortunately the train of empties is light enough that the engine will not have to work too hard as it negotiates seven curves while ascending the hill. *(Joe Collias)*

ABOVE - Train 22 with Lima built F4 2-8-2 552 accelerates north out of Oakford in the mid-1950's. Train 22 left Springfield at 10:00AM daily except Sunday, handling all of the local business in almost every town along the way. Originally #22 ran only to Pekin, but its schedule was extended to the P&PU yard at East Peoria when time freights #44-47 were deleted from the schedule in the late 1940's. Trains #22 and 23 had assigned crews that were not drawn from the Chain Gang. The regular crews had an intimate knowledge of the railroad and businesses along the way. They knew the customers expectations, the spotting locations for cars, and the daily procedures that made efficient operation of the train possible. *(Joe Collias)*

45

ABOVE - Train #6 briefly disturbs the peaceful quiet of Oakford as 4-4-0 #500 eases to a stop on May 20, 1952. The engine will be serviced as the mail and express is exchanged by the RPO crew. Oakford's depot housed a train order office that was open 24 hours a day, except on Sunday. The senior agent at Oakford was Clarence Stroh, who held this position for over a generation. Mr. Stroh was responsible for training newly hired operators for service in C&IM depots. The large yellow water tank was one of two located between Havana and Springfield. If an engine needed more coal the crew would have to wait until the train arrived at Quiver Yard for refueling. *(Robert F. Collins, Morning Sun Books Collection)*

ABOVE - There will be an extended stop at Oakford as the engine crew searches out the source of a problem that has drawn their concern. Conductor Art McDow shares his concerns with local officials as the engine crew peers under the valve gear. Baldwin built two A1 class 4-4-0's in 1927, the year after the C&IM acquired the mainline north of Springfield. The A1s' 64" drivers easily allowed them to keep the short passenger trains on the 2-hour, 20-minute schedule on the run to Pekin. *(Robert F. Collins, Morning Sun Book Collection)*

ABOVE - The prime mover of SD18 61 echoes off the grain silos of the McFadden Elevator as it leads a southbound Expediter through Oakford on February 20, 1995. The train is crossing Center St. and is passing the now-abandoned brick depot. After regular passenger service ended, this small brick depot replaced the original wooden structure. Today SD9 52, normally the remote control unit at Havana, is being brought to Shops dead in tow for maintenance. The C&IM frequently rotated their engines, which is why they were in such good shape. C&IM's diesel mechanics were meticulous in the care and maintenance of the engines. *(Paul Fries)*

ABOVE - The day is warm and clear as 2-10-2 758 leads a Quiver Turn through the gentle farm land south of Oakford. The train is beginning to ascend the 2-mile long grade between Oakford and Atterbury that rises to 1.04% immediately after leaving Oakford. C&IM coal trains of the 1950's typically included a combination of 50-ton two-bay hoppers and 70-ton coal gondolas. Although a Quiver Turn normally hauled 60 loads north to Havana, the C&IM began running 72-car trains in the mid-1950's. A train of 72 empties returning to the Taylorville Division would hardly tax the power of 758, but on the trip north a larger train required the crew to triple Petersburg Hill.

(Robert F. Collins, Morning Sun Books Collection)

ABOVE - Running south of Oakford on a cold winter day in the early 1950's, Extra 758 South gains speed on level, tangent track. In a few minutes the train will arrive at Hill Top. The engineer will cut back on the throttle as the train reduces speed to 25mph to descend into the village of Petersburg. *(John Harrigan, Merlyn Lauber Collection)*

BELOW - Hilltop siding is located at milepost 63, halfway between Atterbury and Petersburg. Southbound freight trains ran up a brief 1.14% grade to the top of the hill, which crested in the middle of the siding. Engine 758 is tugging hard on the southbound Quiver Turn as it hits the top of the hill on May 14, 1955.
(Robert F. Collins, Morning Sun Books Collection)

ABOVE - The cool, crisp afternoon air is filled with smoke and cinders as C&IM G4 class 2-10-2 656 yanks a cut of coal loads out of the siding at Hilltop as it reassembles its train after doubling the hill from Petersburg. Northbound Quiver Turns normally carried up to 60 loads of coal to Havana. The 656 was purchased from the Wabash in 1947. Slightly larger than the C&IM's own 600 class 2-10-2's, the Wabash engines were eclipsed by the larger 2-10-2's acquired from the ACL in 1951 and 1952. The ACL engines could run 60 mph, while the former Wabash engines were limited to 45 mph. The ACL engines also generated 9,000 more pounds of tractive effort than the Wabash engines. This is March 28, 1953. *(James P. Shuman)*

ABOVE - In the late 1950's it was common to see engine consists like this hauling coal trains up the grade at Petersburg. It is August 28, 1993 and the SD38-2's have been leased to the SP. Traditional engine consists have returned as SD9's 50 and 54, spliced by SW1200's 23 and 21, are moments from reaching Hilltop with a CSX coal train for Havana. During the summer of 1993, flooding seriously disrupted river and rail traffic in the Midwest, and rail detours became a common sight. This train originated at Golden Oak Mining Company's Kodak Tipple, located in Charlene, Kentucky. The train was delivered to the Midland at Springfield via the Gateway Western, and is headed to the Havana Coal Transfer Plant for Illinois Power. The coal was either barged a short distance to IP's Havana Plant, or sent up-river to IP's Hennepin Plant. Along with CSX coal, the Midland also handled coal trains from Norfolk Southern and Southern Pacific for Illinois Power until the fall of 1993. *(James Lewnard)*

ABOVE - Shortly after 7:30AM on May 21, 1952 passenger train #6 ascends Petersburg Hill with its typically short consist. Petersburg sits in a shallow valley along the Sangamon River 21 miles north of Springfield. The Springfield and Northwestern constructed the main line running through Petersburg in 1874. Trains leaving Petersburg northbound faced a 1.37% grade that briefly increased to 1.64% just before the south siding switch at Hilltop. Southbound trains faced a 1.08% climb to the siding at Tice.
(Robert F. Collins, Morning Sun Books Collection)

BELOW - A Quiver Turn follows #6 up Petersburg Hill on May 21, 1952. Coal trains doubled the hill from Hurst siding south of Petersburg to Hilltop. The four-mile operation normally consumed an hour. Lima built H1 class 2-10-2 701 leads a cut of approximately thirty 70-ton coal gons that will be set out on a 36-car doubling track. A crossover in the middle of the 96-car Hilltop siding allowed crews to triple the hill if necessary. It also permitted the crews to meet opposing trains while reassembling their own train without fouling the main for excessive amounts of time.
(Robert F. Collins, Morning Sun Books Collection)

RIGHT - Freight trains were restricted to 25 mph from Hilltop through Petersburg to Hurst siding. Extra 753 South glides down the hill with a merchandise train in the mid-1950's. After stopping at Pekin to pick ups cars a merchandise train would normally run to Springfield in 3½ hours, stopping only to take on water at Oakford or Petersburg. Occasionally they would also have a setout for Havana, but short destination cars would more typically be moved by local trains #22/23.
(Joe Collias, Richard Wallin Collection)

ABOVE - A locomotive consist any EMD fan would love: SD18 61, SD20's 80 and 81 and SD9 50 lead an empty Kincaid coal train up the 1.64% Petersburg Hill grade on June 15, 1996. By this point in time the locomotives and the train crews were being taxed because of the larger tonnage trains running the entire length of the line, especially after the sale of the 70 series SD38-2's to UP in 1995. The blue hoppers behind the locomotives are in dedicated slag service between Powerton and Reed Mineral at Sicily. Interestingly, some of the money acquired from the sale of the SD38-2's was used to purchase the blue hoppers for this service. The blue hoppers will be set out in the B Yard at Powerton and the empty coal cars will be set out at Crescent Yard for the UP. *(Scott Muskopf)*

RIGHT - Extra 753 North rolls around a gentle curve between Athens and Tice in the mid-1950's. Athens was a small rural community that had a daytime train order office, an 83-car siding, and a large grain elevator. Passing sidings in the steam era on the Springfield division ranged in length from 60 to 96 cars, just about the size of a normal coal train. The sidings south of Havana were spaced 5 to 9 miles apart, making meets with opposing trains relatively easy to complete. *(Joe Collias)*

BELOW - SD18's 61 and 60, assisted by SD9 53, lead a KISNC (Kincaid-Skyline Mine, Utah-empties) through the 69-car siding at Barr on August 20, 1995. The units will cut off, run around the train, and eventually deliver it to Southern Pacific at Ridgely Tower in Springfield. To the right are the Barr interchange tracks, designated Storage #1 and Storage #2. Built in the early 1970's to facilitate the interchange of 60-car Monterey Mine coal trains received from the CNW, each track held eighty-four 100-ton coal hoppers or gondolas. The Barr interchange was also used for the exchange of 100 cars of potash for Tabor Grain at Havana in 1989. *(Scott Muskopf)*

ABOVE - Barr was an important junction for the C&IM throughout its history. After the Monterey coal trains stopped running, the Midland continued to deliver Pillsbury boxcar traffic going to destinations such as Belvidere, Illinois, and roofing granules from Sicily. The Midland also picked up loads of wheat and sugar destined for the Pillsbury plant in Springfield. In later years the most important traffic exchanged at Barr was garbage, which began on January 24, 1991.

It's April 17, 1993 and the Noon Shops Roadswitcher has arrived at Barr to pick up loaded boxcars of garbage from the CNW. SW1200 22 will couple on and shove the cars out the north end of the #1 Storage track, and proceed south to Shops. The garbage will be forwarded to Christian County Landfill at Callaway by the Mine Run running south of Springfield. *(Don Woodworth)*

ABOVE - North Western-style signals guard the Barr interlocking in 1979 as the CNW agent walks out of the train order office. The CNW was a late arrival to Southern Illinois, building its main line across the Springfield & Northwestern, a C&IM predecessor, in 1913. Until August 7, 1963 a brick tower (BX) guarded the crossing, but it was destroyed in a spectacular wreck when a CNW freight ran through a C&IM freight. The interlocker was eventually automated. To the left of the crossing a loaded Monterey train of C&IM Thrall gondolas waits to be forwarded to Powerton by an Extra North crew from Shops. After the UP abandoned the North Western mainline south of Barr in November 1998, UP trains from South Pekin to St Louis used the former C&IM from Barr to Ridgely Tower in Springfield.
(C&IM Ry., C&IM Chapter NRHS Collection)

ABOVE - White flags fly in the wind as extra 700 south briefly disturbs the peaceful village of Cantrall on a warm summer day in the mid-1950's. Cantrall sits a little less than two miles south of Barr, surrounded by corn and soybean fields. Built by Lima in 1931, the 700's were heavier than the ACL 2-10-2's that were purchased in the early 1950's, but produced slightly less tractive effort than the ACL engines. The 700's were well-respected by the engine crews. They were capable of handling a merchandise train at 60 mph or a large coal train at 40 mph. *(Joe Collias)*

ABOVE - On March 16, 1991, Extra 71 South roars through the countryside between Cantrall and Andrew with connection cars for Shops. Minutes ago this crew set out a HVBBX (Havana-Black Butte-Empty) train to the CNW at Barr, which was an unusual routing. For a brief period a dispute between the CNW and P&PU led to a rerouting of empty CNW coal trains south to Barr, where the trains reversed direction and returned north to South Pekin. When the Manito Roadswitcher operation began the Midland still relied on the Extra North to deliver Peoria cars from Shops at least three days a week. Early on, the connecting traffic from Shops was set out at Havana, but later it was interchanged with the Manito Job at Union Siding. The Extra North also handled coal trains from the P&PU double track to Havana and Powerton as needed, occasionally returning empty trains if a Manito-based crew was not available. *(James Lewnard)*

ABOVE - Only one railroad on the planet could assemble a locomotive consist like this! Rough-looking SD9 50 leads RS1325's 31 and 30 and SD9 54 as they head up a northbound Havana coal train at Andrew on September 12, 1993. Originating on the Southern Pacific in Utah and handed off to C&IM at Ridgely Tower, this was one of the very few SP coal trains way-billed to Illinois Power via the Havana Coal Transfer Plant. C&IM is lending Illinois Power a helping hand during the flood of 1993 when they could not receive coal via barges on the Illinois River. Interestingly, C&IM handled four test trains for Illinois Power in January 1990. These trains originated on Union Pacific at Medicine Bow Mine near Hanna, Wyoming, and were symboled MBHVC (Medicine Bow-Havana-Coal). *(Ryan Crawford)*

ABOVE - Five months have passed since C&IM became another fallen flag, but all seems normal on July 18, 1996. The Shops Roadswitcher, with SW1200 18, spots cars at Solomon Grinding, on Springfield's far north side. Solomon Grinding, also known as Water Works, periodically received hopper cars of iron ore to produce paint coloring. By the early 1990's the ore came from Cleveland Cliffs Iron Mine, located on the Lake Superior & Ishpeming at Eagle Mills, Michigan. It was forwarded to Illinois Central at Chicago, for delivery directly to Shops Yard. The CNW also delivered ore from the Upper Peninsula of Michigan to the C&IM at Barr for Water Works. *(Gary Helling)*

SPRINGFIELD

ABOVE - Extra 751 North exits the double track Springfield main as it enters the limits of Ridgely interlocking in the mid-1950's. Peabody coal maintained two mines in Springfield. Mine #57 sat in the middle of town alongside the joint B&O/IC tracks south of Avenue Tower. Peabody #59 mined the area north of town with service provided by the Springfield Terminal Railway. Both of these mines provided considerable tonnage to the C&IM over the years until they were closed in 1951/52. *(Richard Wallin)*

ABOVE - Former Wabash 2-10-2 656 guides a Short Turn through Ridgely interlocking in the winter of 1952. Short Turns that were based in Springfield brought empties from Barr and Andrew sidings north of Springfield to the mines on the Taylorville Division. Typically a Springfield Short Turn ran as far south as Humphrey, which had a 230-car siding. Frequently the engines were turned at Cimic before continuing to the mines. It was common practice for C&IM steam engines to run backwards with their trains while serving the mines. After delivering empties to sidings near the mines, the Springfield Short Turn crew reversed the process, picking up loads and running north to position the cars for further movement by Quiver Turns or Powerton coal extras. *(Joe Collias)*

ABOVE - SD9 51, SD18 60 and SD38-2 73 pull an Extra North through Ridgely interlocking in the spring of 1975. Upon arrival at Barr the train will pick up 60 loads of coal for Powerton from the CNW interchange. The three-car consist of the train clearly demonstrates the changes in Commonwealth Edison's priorities that led to a significant rethinking of the role of the C&IM in the utilities' operations. In 1964 the C&IM's management was told to discourage interline merchandise traffic, although the C&IM continued to serve on-line businesses. Through train service to Peoria was discontinued in 1968, and the majority of local carload business was delivered to connections at Springfield or Pekin. At the same time, Commonwealth Edison built a power plant in Kincaid Illinois that consumed the majority of Mine #10's coal production. Coal shipments to Havana significantly decreased as direct service coal trains replaced the transfer of coal into barges on the Illinois River. After 1967 train service north of Havana fell significantly. *(Richard Ward)*

ABOVE - On April 7, 1984, SD18 60, SD38-2 72 and RS1325 30 rumble over the ICG diamond at Ridgely Tower and head toward Havana. Today's train includes repaired coal cars being returned to the CNW and BN at Pekin, as well as C&IM Thrall gondolas that have been leased to other railroads. Extra units were operated on days that two SD's were exchanged for two units assigned to Havana or Powerton. Upon arrival at Havana, the Extra North will pick up an empty coal train and forward it to the double track at Pekin. Ridgely was an important interchange point for C&IM. Along with cars way-billed for local delivery, C&IM and GM&O/ICG also interchanged coal trains from Captain Mine at Percy, Illinois that went to Havana and Powerton in the late 1970's and early 1980's. *(Trey Kunz)*

59

ABOVE - In the spring of 1964 B&O FA2 4028 leads two EMD F7b's past WR (Ridgely) Tower on the north side of Springfield. During the 1960's and 1970's B&O freights originated and terminated in GM&O's Ridgely yard on the north end of Springfield. The trains used the C&IM double track main from Ridgely to IC's Avenue Tower on Springfield's east side, where the B&O's line to Decatur and Indianapolis headed east. In later years the puzzle switch in front of the interlocking was removed, and trains were interchanged on the Dick lead which sits on the west side of the interlocking. *(Richard Wallin)*

ABOVE - Freshly overhauled and repainted SD20 82 leads two elderly units, SD9 54 and SD18 60, past Ridgely Tower's northbound home signal on February 11, 1996 to pick up a coal train from the SP. Utah to Kincaid coal train operations began on November 10, 1994. The common practice for the C&IM power was to couple on to loaded slag cars at Shops Yard that were destined to Reed Mineral at Sicily. Shoving the slag hoppers toward Ridgely Tower, the units would add the cars to an awaiting SP coal train bound for Kincaid Station. The SP coal train arrived earlier from St. Louis, pulled through the Dick Lead connection and entered the C&IM main line north of the interlocker. After the Midland units tied on to the south end of the train, the SP power assisted the C&IM units up Ridgely Hill. *(James Lewnard)*

ABOVE - On October 29, 1995, SD9 53, SD18 60, SD9's 52, 54 and RS1325 30 lead a train of loaded covered hoppers past the B&O's ancient tilting target signal that once guarded the crossing of the B&O north of Shops Yard. The signal, a Springfield relic for many years, stood in place until 2004. A wye track here once facilitated movements for B&O trains, but in later years the Midland used the south leg of the wye and the diamond to serve BHM Lumber on the B&O track. The switch crew made their delivery to BHM Lumber after the signal was manually set to horizontal position by a crewman. Today's train has covered hoppers laden with wheat that were picked up at Peoria and way-billed to the Cargill flour mill. The railroad often handled 50-car blocks of wheat for the Springfield mill. Since Cargill could only accept 30 cars at a time for unloading, the extra loads were set out at Andrew Siding for later delivery to Cargill by another train. *(James Lewnard)*

ABOVE - SD38-2 74, SD18 60, and SD38-2 70, are moments from knocking down the home signal at Shops Tower on March 9, 1991. This crew swapped engines and freight cars with the Manito Roadswitcher during the wee hours of the morning, and will soon yard their train and tie up. The yellow Railbox car is loaded with lumber for the Lumber Transfer Yard, which was established in 1989. The Lumber Transfer Yard was one of C&IM's innovative ideas to supplement decreasing coal tonnage during the early 1990's. To the right is one of the railroad's unique, non-operative approach signals that were put in place after the automatic block signal system was removed. The signals are constantly lit, and the blades are permanently set in the approach position. *(James Lewnard)*

ABOVE - On April 2, 1992 engine 75 leads SW1200 23 (dead in tow) into the yard at Springfield with a southbound Expediter. By the summer of 1984 the double track between Avenue Tower and Ridgely Tower was reduced to a single main. Today's train has two gondolas picked up at the Havana House Track, along with bad order BN coal hoppers. C&IM relied heavily on foreign coal car repair as a source of revenue. Coal hoppers and gondolas of all types could be found in the yard at Springfield either awaiting repair or a return trip on the Extra North. *(James Lewnard)*

ABOVE - The Baltimore & Ohio used the C&IM as a belt line for many years to access Ridgely Yard via Avenue Tower. After a trestle collapsed on the B&O east of Springfield in late 1981, trains from Decatur with ICG connecting traffic were rerouted onto Norfolk & Western's Springfield District from Decatur to Shops Tower. At Shops Tower they crossed the interlocker and backed through the C&IM/NW connection track to ICG's Ridgely Yard. By this time the light tonnage warranted only a single, 2nd generation unit. On November 15, 1983, an inbound B&O GP40 shoves northward on C&IM's main line, passing Springfield's famous Lanphier Park.

(Trey Kunz)

ABOVE - From August 17 to August 21, 1992 the Mine Run detoured over Norfolk Southern from Springfield to Taylorville via Decatur when the rail on the 4th St. viaduct in Pawnee was knocked out of alignment by a large cement truck. The detour meant long days for the Mine Run crew as the train made its way east to Decatur, turned, and was sent down the NS Brooklyn District (the St. Louis Line) to Taylorville. On August 20, 1992 engines 23 and 31 back their train of roofing granules and empty garbage boxcars on to the NS/C&IM connection track, which allowed them to enter home rails and deliver their train to Shops Yard. *(James Lewnard)*

ABOVE - Shops Tower guards the crossing of the Norfolk & Western, formerly Wabash, at the north end of Shops Yard in January 1981. The tower still stands today, housing the interlocking equipment operated by the Illinois & Midland's Peoria dispatcher. The tall tower to the right is a mirror tower, which allowed the tower operator to see a train entering the south end of the yard. On Saturday, June 13, 1987, operator Tom Marcellus handed up what would be the last set of flimsies to Extra 72 North. The next day, Stations and Special Instructions #7 took effect, and the dispatcher began issuing track permits to all C&IM trains. By 1989 the tower was closed and operations were moved to the dispatcher's office a couple hundred feet away. *(Railscene by Steve Rippeteau)*

63

ABOVE - C&IM's modern Springfield depot basks in the sunlight on October 27, 1990. For years the C&IM and its predecessors used Union Station (Illinois Central) located on Madison St. in the center of town. Even though the downtown depot made connections for passengers convenient, the Midland opted to build this depot at the north end of Shops Yard in 1937. From an operating standpoint the North End location was better suited to the railroad's needs because of its close proximity to car and locomotive servicing facilities. In later years the station was used for company offices. It was razed in September of 2007. *(James Lewnard)*

ABOVE - On May 8, 1953 the C&IM discontinued it last passenger trains. Company officials have joined the crowd of local citizens to mark the occasion as the train crew examines its final set of train orders before heading north to Pekin. Engineer Peter Higgins and conductor Art McDow chat with chief train dispatcher F.B. Eckard before the train's departure. *(C&IM photo, Martha Smith Collection)*

ABOVE - An extra coach has been added to #6 for the final run. The last passengers are boarding as the RPO crew prepares for the train's departure. Russell Ullery was the mail clerk and John Balsinger was the express messenger. In the last years of passenger service the C&IM maintained six heavy-weight passenger cars originally built in 1927, including two 30' RPO baggage cars, three coaches, and one baggage coach. *(C&IM RY. photo, Martha Smith Collection)*

BELOW - Train #6 heads north on the double track main as an 0-8-0 awaits a signal from Shops tower to reenter the yard and resume switching. The coaches have far more passengers than normal as local citizens and enthusiasts make the last run to Pekin. The train will use the double track main from Shops to Ridgely Tower.

(C&IM Ry. photo, Martha Smith Collection)

65

ABOVE - On October 15, 1983, RS1325 31 and caboose 74 clank across the N&W diamond with a shuttle run returning from Havana. When the C&IM began using pool power on Havana coal trains, a Chain Gang crew was driven to Havana Yard, where they boarded the pool units to move the empty and loaded coal trains between Havana and the P&PU double track. In 1982 this operation was modified. Chain Gang crews began using an engine, usually an RS1325, and a caboose to make the 46-mile run to Havana. At Havana, using a three-unit set of SD's assigned to the Havana yard job, they moved the empty and loaded coal trains to the P&PU. They then returned to Springfield with the shuttle engine. By September 1987 the shuttle runs ended. The Extra North, using three SD38-2s, once again ran from Springfield through Havana to the P&PU, handling all the local freight as well as the Havana coal trains. *(Trey Kunz)*

ABOVE - In 1990 the railroad made operational changes to reduce transit time and locomotive usage. As of May 22, the Mine Run crew, which handled all business on the Taylorville division, was reassigned from Taylorville to Shops Yard. The Mine Run was available to switch the Pillsbury (Cargill) mill in the morning. On the morning of July 18, 1992, the 8:30 AM Mine Run crew switches out flour cars at the north end of Cargill Mill. Behind the silos inside the building were the sugar pits. Behind the covered hoppers was the North End Mill Yard, which loaded boxcars with everything from baking flour to pancake and pie crust mix. *(James Lewnard)*

ABOVE - On September 16, 1988, Extra 74 North waits for the highball from the carmen before it departs out of the north end of the A Yard for Havana and East Peoria. Today's train includes Penn Central boxcars loaded with bagged flour and Conrail covered hoppers of roofing granules going to Conrail at East Peoria. The Pillsbury Mill stands in the background. In the 1950's Pillsbury loaded 55 cars and unloaded 35 cars a day.

In 1988 the Midland used eight locomotives to handle its daily operations. This included one RS1325 (Mine Run), three SD38-2's (Extra North), one SW1200 (PM Shops Road Switcher), and two SD38-2's and a SD18 combo for the (Powerton Job). One SD18, one SD38-2, one RS1325 and four SW1200's were held as spare units. Four of the SD9's were stored serviceable, with 51 being retired.

(Steve Smedley, Ryan Crawford Collection)

ABOVE - Freshly repainted Gateway Eastern GP38 2000 and Gateway Western GP40 3020 prepare to lead train RHSP (Roodhouse-Springfield) out of C&IM's B Yard and head north to the SP connection at Ridgely on June 15, 1993. This blue GP38 was the only unit painted for GWWR's subsidiary Gateway Eastern, which assumed operations of the former New York Central (CR) mainline from East St. Louis to East Alton, Illinois. The GWWR used the C&IM main line to reach the other railroads in Springfield. Today's RHSP picked up and set out to the IC and C&IM. It will interchange with SP before returning to Roodhouse via the GWWR's (ex-GM&O) Airline District. *(James Lewnard)*

ABOVE - By late 1994 the frequent operation of the Kincaid coal trains allowed the railroad to make some operational changes. The coal trains running on the Taylorville Division began to handle local business as well as the coal traffic. On September 23, 1995, SD9 54, RS1325 31, SD18 60 and SD9 53 set out covered hoppers of roofing granules at Shops Yard before proceeding north to deliver the empty train to Southern Pacific. The crew will then return to Shops engine light and tie up. From a railroad standpoint, this was an efficient move, but the local motorists were unhappy about not being able to get around the 6,000-foot coal trains that blocked several grade crossings while the crews made the setout. *(James Lewnard)*

ABOVE - As Commonwealth Edison drastically reduced coal tonnage in the early 1990's, the Midland looked desperately for ways to stay financially solvent. The one "commodity" that single-handedly kept the railroad afloat was garbage! This stinky stuff originated at Star Recycling in Brooklyn, NY, located on the Long Island Railroad. It was routed LIRR-Conrail-CNW-C&IM Barr. Interestingly, one boxcar of garbage produced the same amount of revenue as a car of western coal delivered to the Havana dumper. The railroad's efforts won it Railway Age's coveted Golden Freight Car Award in 1992. On January 7, 1994 the Noon Shops Roadswitcher trundles by the Springfield Depot as it returns from Barr with a block of loaded garbage boxcars. *(Ryan Crawford)*

LEFT - A Quiver Turn led by SD18 60 and two SD9's enter Shops yard in the late summer of 1967. Coal train operations are rapidly changing as Commonwealth Edison's Kincaid power plant is now consuming the majority of Peabody Mine #10's production. Coal traffic dropped 50% in short period of time. By the end of the year much of the coal moving south of Springfield originated at Freeman Crown's Farmersville operation, which shipped coal to Powerton or Havana until 1971. The Farmersville mine is located south of Cimic on the Illinois Central Chicago to St. Louis mainline. The Illinois Central delivered coal to Cimic for interchange to the C&IM. The coal was picked up by a Quiver Turn or a Short Turn for movement north. *(Terry Cook)*

ABOVE - "Kick 'em 22" rattles over the radio as the Noon Shops Roadswitcher crew works the north end of the A Yard on April 17, 1993. Except for a three-year period from May 1990 to June 1993, SW1200's were always assigned to the yard duties at Shops. By 1984 normal operations called for one yard crew at least five days a week. The crew normally worked in the late evening. Extra switch jobs could be called if there was more business at Pillsbury. Routinely, this job spotted the mill and the rip tracks, weighed cars, and set up the Extra North and the Mine Run. It also delivered daily connection traffic. In 1989, a modified union agreement replaced the Shops yard engine with the Shops Roadswitcher, allowing the crew to run beyond yard limits to pick up and deliver CNW interchange traffic at Barr. *(Ryan Crawford)*

ABOVE - The versatility of C&IM's diesel fleet is demonstrated by the power on a Short Turn passing the northbound Shops home signals in the spring of 1973. The four units pulling Extra 30 North provided approximately the same power as three SD9's. In 1960 the C&IM purchased two EMD RS1325's, using them as needed in road or switching service. Heavy coal traffic frequently required the use of SW1200's to supplement the small fleet of SD9's and SD18's. By 1973 the movement of coal from mine #10 at Ellis to Havana or Powerton had significantly decreased, and the SD's were primarily used on the north end of the railroad. *(Terry Cook)*

ABOVE - The Chicago, Peoria, and St. Louis constructed Shops Yard in Springfield in 1895. Located slightly more than a mile northeast of the Illinois state capitol, the yard included a roundhouse and a car repair shop. The sale of the CP&StL Peoria main in 1926 included the yard facilities in Springfield, which the C&IM expanded and modernized. A double track mainline ran through the middle of the yard, stretching from Ridgely tower on the north side of town to Avenue Tower on the east side. The yard was divided into two sections.

The A Yard sat in front of the roundhouse and rip tracks, while the B Yard sat in front of the immense Pillsbury flour mill. Constructed in 1929, the Pillsbury flour mill paralleled the yard's southwest side, providing as many as 100 carloads a day for the C&IM to deliver. By June 4, 1952 the C&IM had collected a large number of 2-10-2's on the rip tracks. As the Taylorville Shop modernized the former ACL 2-10-2's and placed them in service, several of the older Wabash 2-10-2's were set aside. *(C&IM Ry., Martha Smith Collection)*

ABOVE - Old Glory flaps in the breeze on a warm summer morning in June 1960, as freshly repainted hopper 6070 sits in front of the Springfield Paint Shop. In the foreground is the pile driving apparatus for steam crane X41. The Shop facility included in order from front to back: the paint shop, sand blast shop and car shop. The car shop and paint facilities were built when the shops were relocated from Taylorville in 1956.

(Emery Gulash, Morning Sun Books Collection)

BELOW - In June 1960, some equipment lays over on the tidy Rip Tracks at Shops. Boxcar X81 is coupled to gondola X34 and the kitchen car for the wreck train. The boxcar and gondola held extra tackle for the X32 wrecker crane. These cars went out together with the X32 if the wrecker gang had to work long hours cleaning up a railroad-related mess. The cars pictured here were accompanied by the X117, the C&IM's only bunk car.

(Emery Gulash, Morning Sun Books Collection)

ABOVE - A Short Turn crew assembles its train in the B yard in the mid-1950's. Some of the Short Turn crews began their runs in Taylorville, picked up loads from the mines and ran to Springfield. At Shops Yard they exchanged loaded cars for empties before their return home. Since Taylorville Short Turns ran in level territory, their trains were normally larger than Quiver Turns. After the time freights were discontinued south of Springfield, the Short Turns also handled the merchandise cars to Taylorville. The 600 series 2-10-2's were well-suited to the work required, setting out and picking up cars as they worked the line. Empties were set out at five high capacity sidings on the return trip to Taylorville.

(Joe Collias, Richard Wallin Collection)

ABOVE - C&IM D2 class 0-8-0 541 works the B Yard as a freight prepares for departure on the northbound main. The side track immediately in front of the yard engine leads to the south end of the Pillsbury mill. After 1949 three 0-8-0's were normally assigned to the Shops yard jobs. Two crews worked on each shift, providing 24-hour service to the Pillsbury Mill and other industries. One crew worked the north end of the yard, while the other crew worked the south end.

(Joe Collias, Richard Wallin Collection)

ABOVE - Milwaukee Road SW1200 635 sits at the south end of A Yard in June of 1960. A significant increase in coal tonnage has stretched the C&IM diesel fleet to the limit. Two RS1325's are on order for delivery in October. The C&IM leased two Milwaukee SW1200's (642) to work at Springfield until the new units were delivered. Although the Milwaukee units were essentially identical to the C&IM SW1200's, the lack of MU connections needed to work in road service ensured that they would be assigned to yard work in Springfield. The C&IM rarely leased other railroads locomotives. In 1954 the C&IM leased Milwaukee Road SD9's 2235 and 2237 to determine the suitability of the EMD's SD9 for C&IM's operations. For one month in 1995 the C&IM tested a Helm leasing SD40 6051 before purchasing the 80 series SD20's from the IC.
(Emery Gulash, Morning Sun Books Collection)

BELOW - It's Saturday, October 3, 1992 and the Extra 2:00PM Shops Roadswitcher prepares to spot a double plug door boxcar to the south end of Cargill Mill. Interestingly, 22 has replaced the RS1325 that was normally assigned to switch Shops Yard during this period. This day's extra job only worked for two and one half hours, demonstrating the importance of Cargill's business. The south end of the mill had several tracks which had to be spotted in exact order of placement. The yard engine would spend a great deal of time here placing and pulling cars of feed, middlings, screenings, flour and replacing the same with empties. The damage-free boxcar will go inside the building and be spotted at one of Cargill's interior platforms, to be loaded with huge bags of baking flour on pallets. This time sensitive boxcar traffic made up a large percentage of C&IM's line haul business to Peoria. *(James Lewnard)*

ABOVE - On April 22, 1987 the Mine Run from Taylorville is negotiating ICG/GM&O trackage through Springfield to bypass a derailment on the ICG main line between Brickyard Jct. and Avenue Tower. Engine 30 is about to bang across the NS diamond at Iles Tower as it heads toward Ridgely. Even though moves such as this were rare, it was easily handled through the complex track layout running through Springfield. The engine crew this day is Engineer Dolph A. Guy Jr., and Fireman Dolph A. Guy III. Members of the Guy family were engineers on the Midland from CP&STL days through the sale of the C&IM to the I&M, including Dolph Guy Sr., Dolph Guy Jr., Dolph Guy III and Kathy Guy. *(Trey Kunz)*

ABOVE - Making its maiden trip south on January 27, 1996, C&IM 80, the railroad's first SD20, leads SW1200 23 toward Avenue Tower with a short train for Reed Mineral at Sicily. By this time most of the jobs on the Midland have been renamed and reclassified. This job, formerly called the Mine Run, is now simply known as the 84 Shops Roadswitcher. The designation 84 came from the station number for Springfield Shops. The five SD20's, acquired in January 1996, were former IC engines that were attractively painted in a reconfigured lightning stripe scheme. Engine 80 is actually 36 years-old and is beginning its third life. Even at this late date caboose 74 brings up the rear, which was the last caboose to be used in road service on the Midland. *(James Lewnard)*

LEFT - C&IM SD9 50, RS1325 31, and SD18 60 lead a Short Turn out of Shops Yard in the spring of 1970. In two blocks the double track will end and the train will enter the IC main at Avenue. The versatile RS1325 is completely compatible with the two SD's in the locomotive consist. The unit's flexicoil road trucks permit it to operate at the same speed as the SD's, unlike the SW1200's, which were restricted to 35mph in mainline service. *(Richard Ward)*

AVENUE TOWER TO CIMIC VIA THE ILLINOIS CENTRAL

LEFT - Entering the north end of the Avenue interlocking limits, Extra 54 South passes over the C&IM wye as it enters the IC mainline. From 1926 until 1937 C&IM passenger trains used the wye track to access Illinois Central's Springfield station one mile west of Avenue Tower. In 1937 the new C&IM depot opened adjacent to Shops yard and the use of the wye track significantly decreased. The C&IM continued to use the wye track to turn engines, especially after the removal of the turntable at Shops in 1956. *(Ed Johnson)*

RIGHT - On April 16, 1992, the Mine Run pauses at Avenue Tower to lend a helping hand to the crew of the Illinois Central's Springfield Local. Brakeman Jimmy Murray looks on as diesel shop machinist Joe DuBree prepares to hook the locomotive's batteries together with a jumper cable. Once 9542 is cranked up, the Mine Run will continue on its journey toward Cimic and the Taylorville Division. The IC unit will then pick up and deliver to C&IM in Springfield before heading to Mt. Pulaski to interchange cars with the Clinton Local. *(James Lewnard)*

ABOVE - With its handrails decorated for the holiday season, RS1325 30 leads a four-car Mine Run off IC trackage and onto home rails at Avenue Tower on December 29, 1988. Avenue was the largest, most complex junction in Springfield. At Avenue the IC Chicago to St. Louis mainline crossed the B&O Springfield branch (Beardstown to Shawneetown). The B&O and the IC jointly owned the mainline running west to the Springfield passenger station. The B&O Indianapolis to Springfield mainline joined the Springfield Branch just south of the interlocker. The C&IM mainline connected to the IC mainline just north of the tower. A B&O/GM&O industrial line to Ridgely Yard also diverged north at Avenue. By 1990 IC began phasing out Avenue Tower, with one operator working from 9:00AM until 5:00PM. The tower was closed in December of 1992 and the interlocking duties were taken over by the IC's CTC Dispatcher in Homewood, Illinois. *(Scott Muskopf)*

RIGHT and BELOW - The C&IM rarely doubleheaded steam engines on coal trains, but in the mid-1950's 2-10-2's 600 and 602 lead a Short Turn through the Avenue interlocking. Since the IC mainline from Cimic to Avenue would rarely tax the capacity of a single 2-10-2, it is most likely that one of the engines had just received repairs at the Taylorville Shops and is headed back to Springfield for a new assignment. As the engines leave the Illinois Central main they cross the passenger connection track that ran in front of the tower. Illinois Central passenger trains departing Springfield for Chicago used this track to access the northbound main. The second track connected to the joint B&O/GM&O track running north.
(Joe Collias, Richard Wallin Collection)

LEFT - One of the two morning switch crews uses D4 0-8-0 547 to deliver cars to the IC at Avenue yard in Springfield. Deliveries to connecting roads were normally made during the daytime shift. The C&IM brought the cars into Avenue Yard, which was a short distance southeast of the C&IM's yard. Deliveries to the Illinois Terminal were handled through Avenue Yard to the IT's yard, which ran parallel to the IC on the east side of Springfield.
(J. Schmitz, Joe Lewnard Collection)

79

ABOVE - On May 29, 1991, the northbound Mine Run returns from Cimic and clanks through the Avenue Interlocker. It will duck under the Clear Lake Avenue overpass and roll by Avenue Tower. Earlier in the day the Mine Run Crew took both of the RS1325's south along with two cabooses, leaving an engine and caboose at Ellis. The next day the Mine Run will originate at Ellis because the train could not leave Springfield early enough to spot cars at the landfill at 6:00AM. Under a court order, loaded garbage cars could not sit at the landfill for more than 24 hours. *(James Lewnard)*

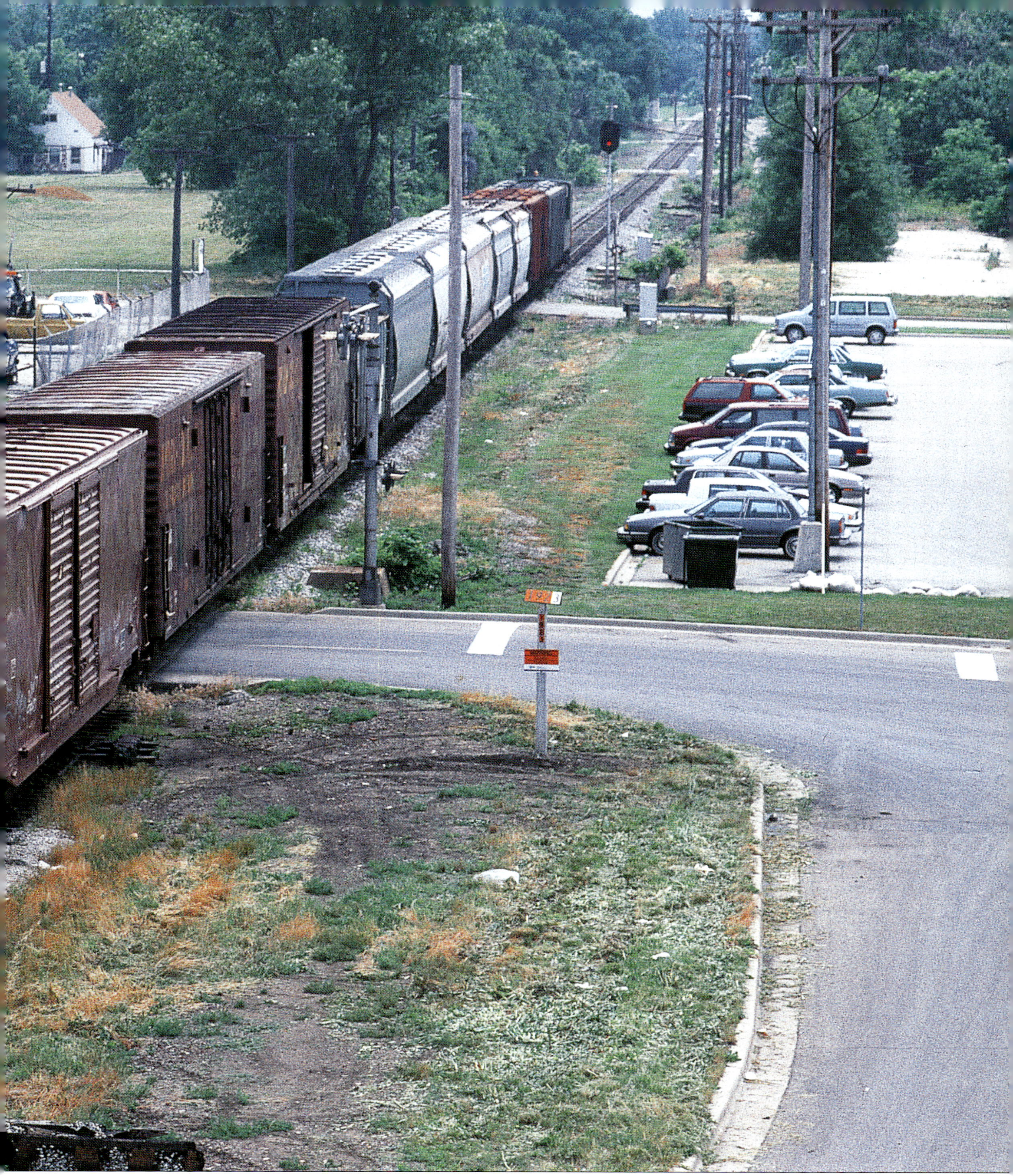

ABOVE - Utilizing trackage rights that the C&IM acquired in 1926, a southbound Short Turn accelerates through the south side of Springfield in the spring of 1970, powered by SD9's 51 and 53 and RS1325 30. The Illinois Central maintained a single track mainline from Avenue through Cimic to a junction with the Litchfield & Madison (later CNW) at Glen Carbon Illinois. The Avenue Tower operator used a CTC system to govern train movements from milepost 191.9 at the tower to the south switch at Divernon Illinois, just short of milepost 211. Although the C&IM trains ran as unscheduled extras, they were not required to display white lights or flags while on the IC. The Illinois Central normally operated four 60 series freights each way from Chicago to St. Louis. By 1970 the IC's passenger trains #21 & 22 no longer operated south of Avenue. *(Richard Ward)*

ABOVE - There isn't a trace of snow on the ground in late 1974 as Extra 74 North approaches the junction with the Baltimore & Ohio's line from Flora on Springfield's south side. The nearly new SD38-2 is assisted by SD9's 52 and 53. Operation of the SD38-2's south of Springfield was relatively rare in the mid-1970's, as most coal moved in unit trains north of Springfield. Although the vast majority of its production was consumed by the Kincaid power plant, Peabody Mine #10 still loaded coal for movement to Havana for other Commonwealth Edison plants. *(Terry E. Cook)*

ABOVE - SD18 60 assists SD9's 54 and 53 as they roll a Quiver Turn through Springfield on the IC main on July 31, 1966. From 1965 until 1971 the C&IM normally ran a Taylorville-based Quiver Turn north in the morning that returned south from Havana in the mid-afternoon. Later in the morning a Springfield-based Short Turn crew headed south to Ellis, returning north in the early afternoon. The Short Turn normally waited for the Quiver Turn in the yard at Springfield before heading south. Although most of the 137 empties on this train will be delivered to Peabody Mine #10 for loading, it has a block of cars to set out at Cimic for delivery to the Freeman Crown mine in Farmersville by the Illinois Central. The speed limit for freight trains south of Springfield was 45mph. *(John Harrigan, Merlyn Lauber Collection)*

82

ABOVE - On February 10, 1987 SW1200 22 leads the Mine Run on its return trip to Taylorville, passing through ICG's Brick Yard Jct. on Springfield's south side. The C&IM frequently leased its Thrall gondolas to other railroads. The Mine Run has Thrall gondolas being returned to storage at Ellis Yard and empty covered hoppers headed for Universal Granule. For many years SW1200's were used on the Mine Run, but in one month an RS1325 began exclusively handling the tonnage on the south end. Engine assignments will change again when garbage trains commence operations on January 24, 1991. The track diverging to the left was a new connection built by the ICG to link the IC and GM&O main lines using the Illinois Terminal Belt Line around the city. *(Trey Kunz)*

ABOVE - Extra 54 South glides across the Sugar Creek bridge in the middle of Lake Springfield on May 21, 1967. The train's 169 cars stretch back to Toronto siding slightly more than a mile north of the lake. Toronto was the only controlled siding between Avenue and Cimic. The siding could hold a 181-car train. Immediately after crossing the Lake the Quiver Turn will climb the only grade of any consequence on its way to Ellis Yard. Three SD9's were rated at 21,000 tons on the southbound run. Empties for the Farmersville mine will be set out at Cimic. An IC local will run south from Avenue at 8AM the next morning to pick up the empties and deliver them to Farmersville, located eleven miles south of Cimic. The Farmersville mine typically loaded 30-40 cars a day. After setting the empties and pulling the loads, the IC local will return to Cimic, setting out the loads for further movement by the C&IM's Quiver Turn. *(Ed Johnson)*

ABOVE - On February 18, 1995 SD18 61 leads three SD9's – 53, 50 and 54 – in as many schemes as they lug an SP coal train up IC's Cotton Hill grade. Today's train consists of brand new five-bay aluminum rapid discharge cars that can be dumped remotely using a second air line connection for that purpose. From 1967 until the contract finally expired in 1992, Peabody Mine #10 was the sole provider of fuel for Com Ed's Kincaid Station. Assuming the presidency of the C&IM in 1989, George Stern worked hard to win the contracts to deliver coal to the Kincaid station. In May and June of 1992, after much effort, twelve test coal trains were delivered to the Kincaid Plant. Two years later the C&IM was awarded a contract to deliver Utah coal to Kincaid. *(Ryan Crawford)*

ABOVE - On September 28, 2000 a beautiful afternoon sun glints off the flanks of SD20's 84 and 80 as they haul a long string of slag loads, destined for Reed Mineral, up IC's .47% Cotton Hill grade. By late 1994 the use of low-sulphur Utah coal depleted Reed Mineral's pile of slag that it used to make roofing granules. At the same time the Powerton Station was having difficulties finding a place to dispose of their slag. To remedy the situation an agreement was reached between the C&IM and Reed Mineral in which the railroad would purchase hopper cars and rebuild the old Ash track at Powerton to load the slag, handling it to Ellis Yard for unloading. Reed Mineral now received and shipped via the C&IM. *(Ryan Crawford)*

LEFT - The northbound Mine Run heads through Glenarm and nears the Old Rt. 66 overpass on July 15, 1987. The white boxcars trailing the engine are unusual because the Mine Run normally handled only roofing granules, home road leaser coal cars and an occasional agricultural load. A connection with the NS at Taylorville was still active during 1987 and probably accounts for the unusual routing of these boxcars. During this period, all trains were limited to 25 mph between Cimic and Brick Yard Jct., due in part to ICG's rough track south of Springfield. By this date, the ICG's St. Louis main line had been scaled back to Farmersville, which Canadian National still operates in 2009. *(Bill Raia)*

BELOW - Three newly acquired SD20's are assisted by an SD18 as they lean into a one degree curve south of Glenarm with train SNKIC (Skyline Mine, Utah-Kincaid-Coal). Most of the coal trains interchanged with SP at Ridgely used older 100-ton steel cars. Many of the cars were lettered for Rio Grande, as well as some second hand BN, UP and Clinchfield hoppers re-lettered for SP subsidiary CTRN (Central Tennessee Railway & Navigation Co.). After these train sets were emptied and returned to SP they were forwarded to the Wisconsin Central at Chicago and loaded with taconite in Minnesota for the return trip to Geneva, Utah. Newer aluminum cars were also used on Kincaid coal trains, but were not used for taconite loading because the aluminum could not withstand the chemical composition and the weight of the taconite. *(Ryan Crawford)*

85

CIMIC TO TAYLORVILLE

ABOVE - It is May 31, 1990 and engine 31 has a five-car Mine Run in check as it slowly rounds the curve off IC trackage at Cimic. The Mine Run is entering the Taylorville Division at C&IM milepost 121. The name Mine Run was a holdover from steam days on the Taylorville Division when several crews per day would switch the mines between Pawnee and Taylorville. In modern times the Mine Run was a truly unique job for several reasons. It was the last job on the railroad to use a caboose, the last job to use a fireman, and the last job to utilize a five-man crew. Aside from using an RS1325 most of the time, it was the last assigned job on the Taylorville Division and the last job to originate at the onetime C&IM headquarters at Taylorville. *(Ed Johnson)*

ABOVE - SD18 61 has the Mine Run tucked safely in the siding at Cimic on June 2, 1992. Today's train is waiting out a meet with Extra 74 South, which is handling one of the twelve test trains from the IC at Avenue Yard to Kincaid Generating Station. Loaded at Old Ben Mine #26 on the Burlington Northern in southern Illinois, these trains were labeled OBKNC, (Old Ben-Kincaid-Coal). Meets like this on the south end were ultra rare in the modern era because for years there was only one train a day! *(James Lewnard, Joe Lewnard Collection)*

ABOVE - On a cold February 1, 1971 SD18 61 assists SD9's 54 and 50 as a Quiver Turn crew arrives at Cimic. The caboose hop will cross the parallel Illinois route 104 and enter Cimic Yard. After picking up the Farmersville coal loads, the crew will contact the Avenue Tower operator for permission to open a set of electrically controlled switches to enter the mainline. After the Avenue operator unlocks the switches, the C&IM crew will throw the switches by hand and head north to Springfield. In a few months a prolonged coal miner's strike will eliminate the need to pickup at Cimic. By the end of the year Freeman Crown will close the mine and hold it out of production for over twenty years. *(Don Woodworth)*

BELOW - In October of 1970 a CNW coal train pulls under the I-55 bridge as it approaches Cimic. The Cimic interchange yard is directly above the coal train. SD18 60, SD9 54 and RS1325 31 will pull into the connection track and await permission to head north to Avenue. Although the Kindcaid power plant consumed up to 10,000 tons of coal every day, Peabody Mine #10 could produce over 19,000 tons per day. The excess coal was frequently shipped to Waukegan and other Commonwealth Edison plants in the Chicago area. *(Dwight A. Smith, Ryan Crawford Collection)*

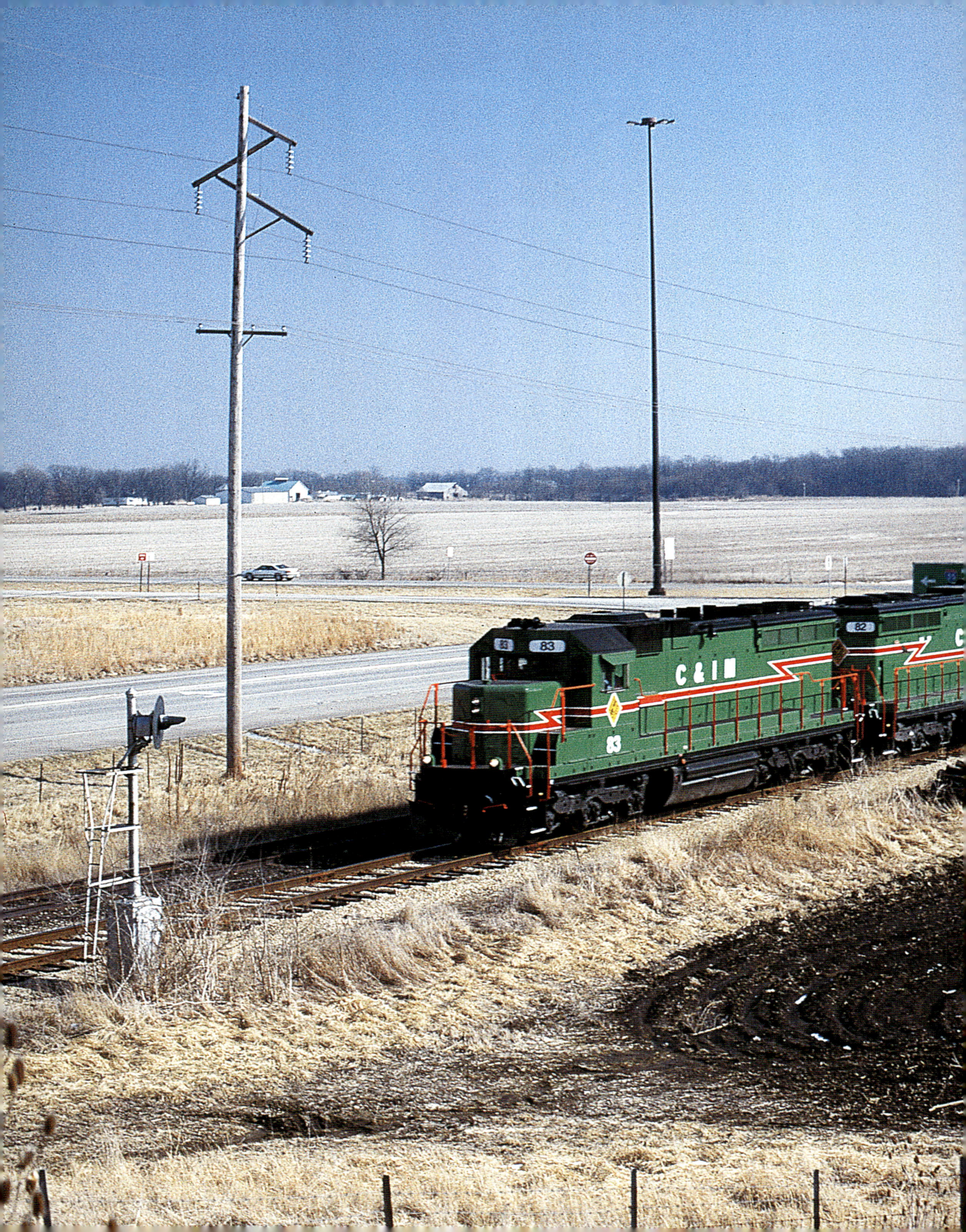
C&IM
83
83
83
82

Although the sale of C&IM to Genesee & Wyoming is now ten days old, this photo strikes up images of big-time railroad publicity. Shining like new pennies, SD20's 83, 82 and 81 lead a brand new set of CTRN four-bay aluminum coal hoppers toward Cimic on February 19, 1996. The train is passing the defunct, non-operative approach signal for the CTC Cimic Interlocker. The signal is exactly 2,341 feet from the junction. Ironically, C&IM's newest locomotives were property of C&IM for only about two or three weeks, but lasted in this livery up until the end of their careers on the Illinois & Midland. Only C&IM 81 remains a part of the I&M locomotive fleet as of late 2008.

(Scott Muskopf)

ABOVE - It's September 4, 1994 and the Mine Run is northbound, geographically west, as it passes milepost 117 on the Taylorville Division at Pawnee. In late March 1993 the Mine Run was rescheduled to depart Shops Yard at 2:00PM instead of the normal 8:30AM call. A late afternoon call enabled them to handle more garbage cars for Five Oaks Landfill. The change increased total weekly placements from 44 loads to 63 loads of garbage per week. The crew inside the cab from left to right is: Brakeman Jimmy Murray, Conductor Jim Burris and Engineer Tommy Matthews. These three gentlemen, along with Dallas Stout (not pictured), used the stove on caboose 74 to heat up the best-tasting home-made apple pie known to man! *(Scott Muskopf)*

ABOVE - A gaggle of C&IM SD's trundles through Pawnee with a coal train for Kincaid on June 15, 1996 at the location of the Pawnee Railway's original depot. In the beginning the Pawnee had one train crew, one dispatcher and one maintenance-of-way employee. Roughly 107 years before this photo was taken, citizens of Pawnee gathered at this location to send the first train west to Glenarm with a single coach pulled by a 4-4-0 steam engine. Today's train is no spectacle to the people of Pawnee, it's just another coal train blocking the crossings as it ambles through town at 10 mph. *(Don Woodworth)*

ABOVE - Engine 31 handles the Mine Run as it heads west (timetable north) over the impressive Horse Creek trestle at Pawnee on October 12, 1987. The original Horse Creek trestle was constructed in 1906. It was 780 feet in length and cost roughly $50,000 to build. Today, the Mine Run is scooting over the newer Horse Creek trestle, which was built in 1948. The construction methods used in the late 1940's made the bridge considerably shorter (225 ft.) because of earth-filled approaches that kept the railroad on the original alignment 30 feet above the creek bed. For many years the speed limit on the Taylorville Division was 30 mph, but by 1991 all trackage through Pawnee was limited to 10 mph. *(Don Woodworth)*

ABOVE - In 1949 Peabody Coal Company began construction of Mine #10 at Ellis Illinois. Limited operations began in 1952, with full production commencing by July 30. In the first year of operation Mine #10 produced up to 13,000 tons of coal per day. By 1960 production had increased to 19,000 tons daily. Equipped with highly efficient machines, Mine #10 quickly replaced four Peabody coal mines located between Kincaid and Taylorville. In 1952 Mine #7 at Kincaid, Mine # 9 at Langleyville, and Mine #58 at Taylorville closed.

Mine #8 at Tovey (Humphrey) closed in 1954. Peabody Coal originally planned to open a new mine #11 at Taylorville, but later cancelled the project. The C&IM built Ellis Yard, which sits in front of Mine #10 in 1949.

Kinney yard was constructed in Taylorville to serve Mine #11, but was primarily used to store empty cars. Viewed from the air on August 22, 1952, Ellis Yard is in full operation.

(C&IM Ry. photo, Martha Smith Collection)

ABOVE - The Ellis depot stands vigil at the west (railroad north) end of Ellis yard on July 17, 1991. This depot was built in conjunction with Ellis Yard to handle the clerical duties associated with the many hoppers and gondolas loaded at Peabody Mine #10. The depot measured roughly 41'x15' and had a nine-foot bay for the operator. It was the largest modern C&IM depot on the Taylorville Division, and between 1952 and 1967 was also one of the busiest. An agent with an army of clerks worked around the clock to ensure Commonwealth Edison that coal would be loaded and ready for shipment to Havana and Powerton. The agency was closed in September 1989, and during its last few years was jointly operated with the Taylorville facility by agent/operator Ed Gibbs. *(Don Woodworth)*

ABOVE - Newly delivered SW1200 18 enters the lead to Mine #10 on May 4, 1955. The mine run crew went on duty at Taylorville earlier in the morning and ran to Ellis to switch the mine. The crew is preparing to pull coal loads from the six track load yard in front of the mine. The loads will be placed in Ellis Yard and assembled into appropriate blocks for delivery to Havana, Powerton, or connecting railroads at Springfield and East Peoria. Some of the coal will be delivered to the Wabash at Taylorville. The crew will also place empties into the empty yard behind the mine. Later in the day mine employees will roll the empty cars into the mine by releasing the handbrakes, allowing the cars to coast into one of the four tipple tracks without the use of a locomotive. *(Tom Ratsch Collection)*

ABOVE - C&IM 60 leads SW1200's 22 and 21 as a Short Turn pulls down the main at Ellis. Earlier in the day a mine run from Taylorville began spotting the empties and pulling the loads from Mine #10. The Short Turn's northbound train is waiting in the yard for the return trip. If the train was ready at Ellis a Short Turn crew could make the roundtrip from Springfield to Ellis and return in three hours.

(Railscene by Steve Rippeteau)

ABOVE - C&IM's two SD18's bracket newly acquired SD20 80 with a westbound (railroad north) empty coal train at Ellis Yard on March 9, 1996. After the train crew inspects the train and completes the terminal air brake test, Extra 60 North will depart for Ridgely Tower and the connection with the Southern Pacific. By March 1995 the Midland was intermittently using SP locomotives on a run-through basis from Ridgely to Ellis yard. However, C&IM power predominated on most coal moves that made the sight of run-through power rare until after the take-over by Genesee & Wyoming. During the 1980's, C&IM used Ellis Yard to store nearly 250 idle coal cars along with the extra cars way-billed to Reed Minerals. By 1990 most of the coal cars were either sold or leased out to other utility companies. *(Richard Ward)*

95

ABOVE - On June 15, 1996 the east end (railroad south) of Ellis yard is a blaze of C&IM color. On the main line engine 84 leads a Powder River Basin coal train from the Union Pacific at Crescent. SD20 82 occupies Ellis #1 track while SD9 53 is laying over on Ellis #2. RS1325 30 sits on Ellis #5 track with cars spotted at the original coal dumper. The original dumper (with car-shaker) was built in April 1992. Amazingly, the railroad built this interim facility in 29 days, just in time to receive 108,000 tons of Illinois coal. After replacement by a new dumper, the original unit was used to unload hoppers of slag from the Powerton Generating Station. This slag is trucked a short distance to Reed Mineral at Sicily, which processes the slag into roofing granules. *(Scott Muskopf)*

ABOVE - In 1994, the Pawnee Transportation Company, a C&IM subsidiary, constructed a new coal dumper at Ellis to unload Utah coal trains for Com Ed's Kincaid Station. Remote control SD9 53 is spotting low-sulfur Utah coal into the new dumping shed. Like the previous unloading facility it was permanently connected to Peabody Mine #10's conveyor belt, which delivered the coal across the highway to the Kincaid plant. To better facilitate the unloading operations the C&IM shop forces fitted five locomotives with remote control between 1992 and 1995, including SD9's 52, 53, 54, RS1325 30 and SW1200 18. These locomotives were easily recognizable by the multi-colored light bracket on the cab. *(Paul Fries)*

ABOVE - The Mine Run switches cars at Ellis on November 12, 1990, directly across Illinois Rt. 104 from Commonwealth Edison's Kincaid Generating Station. Technically, the Kincaid Station was located at Sicily, five miles west of the town of Kincaid. The locations of Ellis and Sicily were adjacent on the C&IM, and only a grade crossing (where the photographer is standing) separates the two. One of the covered hoppers in the Mine Run's consist is N&W 170735, which was typical of the older two-bay covered hoppers that connecting roads provided for roofing granule service. The C&IM did not own covered hoppers suitable for this service. *(Don Woodworth)*

ABOVE - On August 13, 1991 the Mine Run spots empty covered hoppers to Reed Mineral (formerly Universal Granule) at Sicily before departing south with garbage cars for Christian County Landfill. The Reed facility, built in 1985, refined slag from the Kincaid Station into different grades of roofing shingle granules. The first year the facility was open, the C&IM handled 880 cars, and by 1989 that number jumped to a whopping 3,000 carloads annually. Located to the south of Reed's was Midland Soil (behind the anhydrous tanks), which occasionally utilized C&IM service. A few covered hoppers of potassium chloride and diammonium phosphorus were spotted to this facility each year. *(James Lewnard)*

97

ABOVE - A southbound Mine Run charges through Kincaid with garbage for the Christian County Landfill on July 17, 1991. The train consists of three tarped gondolas and a 60' double door boxcar of SP heritage. The boxcars assigned to garbage service were former auto parts cars repainted boxcar red and lettered NSSX and EMAX. They were loaded with 65 semi-compacted 5'x5'x7' long bales of Municipal Solid Waste (MSW). The Conrail gondolas are hauling contaminated soil, which the landfill accepted on occasion. The landfill also accepted sludge, which was handled in blue containers riding on 60' flatcars. The garbage business helped sustain the Taylorville Division until Kincaid Station began receiving low-sulfur Utah coal in November 1994. *(Don Woodworth)*

RIGHT - A late afternoon sun accentuates the lines of RS1325 31, as it and sister 30 spot garbage cars to the Christian County Landfill on April 29, 1993. This is the view that engineer Tommy Matthews had while running the engines from the cab of engine 30. Soon, he will change ends and relocate himself inside the cab of engine 31 for the trip back to Sicily and Springfield Shops. The C&IM constructed the landfill spur in December 1989. The landfill was built on the sight of Peabody Mine #9.

(Ryan Crawford)

ABOVE - On July 17, 1991 the Mine Run shoves boxcars and gondolas through the switch connecting C&IM's main line with the Christian County Landfill spur. Today, veteran conductor Gene "Bug Eye" Anderson tends to the switch. Gene faithfully served the C&IM for nearly 40 years, beginning as a section laborer at Havana in 1955. He became a brakeman, and eventually was promoted to conductor in 1970. The Christian County Landfill was purchased by Waste Management Inc. on May 28, 1992. Waste Management received New York garbage until September 30, 1994. *(Don Woodworth)*

ABOVE - Engines 31 and 30 prepare to spot loads and pull empties at the landfill near Callaway. The engines have just run around their train at Callaway siding located just beyond the boxcars. Callaway was the second passing siding after leaving Taylorville and could hold 39 cars. The landfill could only accept 12 cars at a time for unloading. *(Ryan Crawford)*

ABOVE - On July 14, 1987 RS1325 30 handles four loads of roofing granules to Taylorville and the NS connection. C&IM's connection with the B&O was called Bando (B-and-O), and the Mine Run has just passed through its switch, connecting the C&IM and B&O main lines on Taylorville's west side. Three industries were located on the B&O connection track, which was 7302' long. There was also a B&O Connection Storage Track that held 16 cars. Little to no interchange was conducted at Bando after 1988. The connection switch was spiked and taken out of service in 1994. *(Bill Raia)*

ABOVE - In 1903 Commonwealth Edison and Peabody Coal acquired control of the tiny Pawnee railroad. Renaming the road the Chicago & Illinois Midland, they quickly extended the railroad east to Taylorville. In 1906 the C&IM built a new yard in Taylorville, adding a large repair shop and engine servicing facility in 1907. Sixty-one years later a yard crew switches coal loads at Taylorville. In the busy times of WWII twenty crews worked out of Taylorville Yard. On a normal day two yard crews switched the yard and company shops. They interchanged cars with the Wabash three times a day and exchanged cars with the B&O via the connection at Bando on the west side of town. They also switched Peabody Mine #58 and assembled the 40 series time freights. By 1968 the work at Taylorville had radically changed and the number of assignments had significantly decreased. Crews are now called at 8:45AM or 5:00PM to complete the work of the day. *(Terry Cook)*

LEFT - A rare mileage excursion prepares to depart Taylorville Yard and head toward Pekin on Saturday, September 7, 1991. Organized by Meteor Rail of St. Louis and High Iron Travel of Denver, the excursion was the first passenger train on the C&IM since the railroad hosted the American Freedom Train on July 22, 1977. Today, the passengers will ride as far as Cimic, where they will board buses to Springfield. Concerned about liability issues, the Illinois Central would not allow the passengers to ride the train on its trackage between Cimic and Avenue Tower. After the passengers reboarded in Springfield, the train went to Pekin, turned and eventually tied-up at Springfield Shops. The following day the railroad ran four trips to Havana for employees and their family members. The consist included Wabash Pullman Chief Keokuck, built in 1927, and former Frisco Pullmans Cimarron River and Caritas, both built in 1948. *(Don Woodworth)*

ABOVE - Engines 60, 53 and 51 await the next call to duty at Taylorville on October 4, 1969. Three units sets of SD9's and SD18's are the normal power for the Quiver Turns, which were operated by crews called from the Taylorville Chain Gang. From WWII until the mid-1960's the C&IM operated two to five Quiver turns north to Havana each day. Taylorville was also the home base for the mine run crews, which were called as needed to serve the four Peabody mines located between Taylorville and Ellis. Mine run crews also switched the local industries in the towns between Taylorville and Cimic. They made an occasional run to Auburn or the CNW connection at Compro until the line was abandoned in 1956. After the older mines closed in 1952 and 1954, the primary responsibility of the mine run crews was to switch Peabody #10 in Ellis. As coal traffic on the Taylorville division evaporated in the 1980's, the Quiver turns were discontinued, leaving a lone mine run and an occasional extra to handle all of the remaining business. *(Dave McKay Morning Sun Books Collection)*

ABOVE - RS1325 30, the locomotive assigned to today's Mine Run, idles in front of the Taylorville engine shed on December 29, 1988. Soon the 8:30AM Mine Run crew will hop aboard, pick up caboose 74, and head north to Universal Granule at Sicily. Beyond the engine shed is a house trailer that served as the Taylorville agency for number of years. In 1988 the normal operations called for a carman from Springfield to travel to Taylorville and fire the engine up, as well as ice the coolers in the caboose and engine. The carman then followed the Mine Run to Sicily, where he would make routine car inspections and a terminal air brake test on cars being handled to Shops. The Taylorville agent/operator Ed Gibbs also made the daily jaunt to Sicily and Ellis to assist the Mine Run and give his daily OS for Ellis depot. The Taylorville and Ellis agencies were closed when Ed Gibbs retired in September 1989. *(Scott Muskopf)*

C&IM POWER LEASED TO NEIGHBORING RAILROADS

ABOVE - On January 4, 1991 C&IM SW1200 22 and TP&W GP20 3019 team up to move a grain train off of P&PU trackage and toward the Toledo Peoria & Western's yard in East Peoria. In November 1990, four TP&W GP20's sustained heavy damage in a grade crossing collision. The C&IM helped TP&W remedy the situation by arranging the lease of two locomotives. SW1200's 22 and 23 were delivered to the TP&W on November 23, 1990. Engine 23 did not last long on the Tip Up and was returned to the Midland due to a mechanical failure on December 9. The C&IM replaced unit 23 with SW1200 21 for the remainder of the lease. The C&IM switchers were assigned to the Kolbe Local and switch jobs in TP&W's East Peoria Yard.

(Ed Johnson)

RIGHT - C&IM's SD38-2's roamed the Midwest from late 1977 until early 1983, paying back horsepower hours to the BN and CNW for units used in coal service on the C&IM. On June 16, 1979 two SD38-2's leading a BN freight pass a commuter train powered by upgraded E8a 9903, which has stopped at the Aurora passenger station. Some of the C&IM units will run offline for several years, serving as far as Iowa and Minnesota. *(Richard Ward)*

RIGHT - A BN extra freight powered by C&IM SD18 60 and SD9 51 delivers interchange cars to the Milwaukee Road at Savanna, Illinois on December 9, 1979. Burlington Northern frequently used C&IM power on its mainline to the Twin Cities. After completing the delivery, the train will resume its journey along the Mississippi River north into Wisconsin. *(Larry L. Anglund)*

ABOVE - Three C&IM SD38-2's pull a BN freight from the Peoria line into Galesburg Yard on April 13, 1979. BN restricted the SD38-2's to regional service because their 3,200-gallon fuel tanks limited their operating range. *(Larry L. Anglund)*

ABOVE - An unusual combination of C&IM SD9 51 and BN GP7 1589 wait on the north side of Galesburg to enter the yard on December 9, 1978. C&IM's SD9's were leased to both the BN and the CNW in the late 1970's. As Environmental regulations drastically reduced the use of Illinois coal in Commonwealth Edison's generating stations and as run-through power on units coal trains from the West increased, the C&IM's need to use its own power significantly decreased. On a normal day in the late 70's the C&IM might need to use only six of its 13 EMD SD's. The Midland's well-maintained power was well-suited to the needs of its larger neighbors.

(Larry L. Anglund)

ABOVE - SD9's 51 and 50 maneuver through CNW's South Pekin yard in the late 1970's. Freights from Proviso Yard to Madison yard in the St. Louis area bypassed Peoria, pausing at nearby South Pekin to change crews. The C&IM units could not be used on through freights north of Peoria because they were not equipped with the Automatic Train Control equipment needed to run on the CNW Illinois Division mainline. Thus, they spent most of their time in local service in the Peoria and St. Louis areas while on loan to the CNW. *(Railscene by Steve Rippeteau)*

ABOVE - C&IM RS1325 30 and Keokuk Junction HE15 4253, an ex-CNW Cummins re-powered GP7, switch cars on the KJRY at La Harpe, Illinois on November 21, 1991. In October 1991 the Midland leased the 30 to the Keokuk Junction Railway to supplement power undergoing maintenance work. Engine 30 operated on the KJRY for 17 months before it was finally returned to the C&IM on April 8, 1993. SW1200 18 was also leased to the KJRY for a short time in the early 1990's. *(Hal Collins)*

C&IM POWER ROSTER

ABOVE - Proudly displaying the C&IM distinctive herald on its smokebox, Baldwin built 4-4-0 A1 class #502 waits patiently at Pekin to lead train #7 on its run to Springfield on November 19, 1951. Constructed in 1928, the 502 spent the vast majority of its days shuttling passengers between Springfield and Peoria. The last 4-4-0 constructed for mainline service in America, the 502 had 64" drivers and weighed in at 118,400 lbs. Generating 18,500 pounds of tractive effort, it was capable of sprinting down the mainline at 70mph. On a clear, sunny day the 502 was rated at 1,350 tons north to Petersburg, 450 tons on the hill, and 1,800 tons for the remainder of the trip to Peoria. On the return trip, the 502 could haul 1,800 tons to Kilbourne and 750 tons for the remainder of the trip to Springfield. The 502 and its two sister A1 class engines easily handled the two- to three-car consists of the C&IM passenger trains *(Robert F. Collins, Morning Sun Books Collection)*

ABOVE - Beginning in 1937 the C&IM began to replace aging 2-8-0's and 2-8-2's assigned to switching service with 0-8-0's. The first two engines, D2 class #540 and 541, were built for the C&IM by Lima. During WWII two D3 class 0-8-0's #545-546 were acquired from the Manufacturer's Railway, followed by two D4 class engines, #547-548 from the Kentucky and Indiana Terminal in 1949. In 1953 the C&IM added one more 0-8-0, engine 549, which was also purchased from the K&IT. On September 6, 1953 the 549 waits quietly at Shops for a turn in the yard. The seven 0-8-0's covered the yard jobs in Taylorville, Springfield, and Havana.

(Lawson Hill, Boston Chapter NRHS Collection)

ABOVE - Class F4 2-8-2 550 prepares to couple on to a northbound passenger special which is sitting on the Team Track near the Springfield depot on May 14, 1955. A yard engine will help double the train together before its departure. Lima built two F4's for the C&IM in 1928 (#550-551), and one additional F4 (#552) in 1931. The F4's were versatile engines, equally capable of handling freight or passenger trains, switch jobs or mine runs. At 319,000 pounds, the 550's weighed 20% less than a H1 class 2-10-2. Producing 53,800 pounds of tractive effort, a 550 could roll 7,025 tons on the Taylorville line, 4,800 tons from Springfield to Petersburg, and 1,600 tons up Petersburg Hill. The 550's spent much of their time on way freights 22/23 and switching at Pekin.
(Robert F. Collins, Morning Sun Books Collection)

ABOVE - Former Wabash 2-10-2 654 sits on the turntable lead at Springfield in the early 1950's. Built by Dunkirk in 1917 as Wabash 2517, the G4 class 654 was one of two 2-10-2's acquired by the C&IM in 1942. Between 1941 and 1950 the C&IM purchased nine Wabash 2-10-2's. The G4's were 10% larger than C&IM's own 600 series G1 class 2-10-2's. Both classes lacked booster engines (except for engine 600) and were restricted to 45 mph on the mainline. A 650 could handle only 50 more tons than a 600 on Petersburg Hill, but could handle 600 more tons on level track. With their slower speed, the former Wabash engines spent much of their time on coal trains and mine runs, leaving the fast freight to the more agile 700 series 2-10-2's. *(J. Schmit, Joe Lewnard Collection)*

107

ABOVE - Delivered in the early years of the Great Depression, the four H1 class 2-10-2's proved to be a wise investment. Sturdy and reliable, the 700's shouldered the primary burden of moving both merchandise and coal trains for 24 years. The four Lima built 2-10-2's were capable of moving an 11,000-ton coal train from Taylorville to Shops. The hilly terrain north of Springfield limited the 700's capacity to 6,750 tons, while the run up Petersburg Hill further limited them to 2,200 tons. North of Petersburg, the 700's could handle 8,500 tons all the way to Peoria. On May 14, 1955 H1 701 is ready to leave Shops Yard with a coal train for Havana.
(Robert F. Collins, Morning Sun Books Collection)

RIGHT - At the end of World War II the C&IM elected to deck out its steam engines with a bold red tender stripe and an enhanced company herald. It also enlarged the engine number on the tender, ensuring that every engine could be clearly identified when completing meets with opposing trains. Sitting at the Springfield roundhouse on September 6, 1953, H1 class 702 has an enlarged bunker capable of holding 20 tons of coal. *(Emery Gulash, Morning Sun Books Collection)*

The late afternoon sun illuminates H1 class 2-10-2 703 as she is readied for another run at Springfield. Built by Lima in 1931, the 703 produces 76,500 pounds of tractive effort. Her 64" drivers give her a maximum speed of 60mph. Although she can haul 8,500 tons of freight from Peoria to Kilbourne, Tice Hill and Ridgely Hill limit her to 3,500 tons on the southbound run. *(Joe Collias, Richard Wallin Collection)*

RIGHT - SW1200 18 sits in front of the Pekin engine shed on July 4, 1961. SW1200's 18 and 19 were the first diesels delivered to the Midland in April 1955, and were the only C&IM units purchased from EMD without dual-cab controls. Early modifications to the SW1200's included the addition of a small beacon on the cab roof and one inch white pin-stripes. Legend has it that beacons were added to the SW1200's to discourage the switch crews from hiding and having late night poker games in the Springfield Yard. SW1200's 18 and 19 were put to work immediately, with one handling mine runs and switching on the Taylorville Division and the other assigned to Shops Yard.
(Ryan Crawford Collection)

ABOVE - SW1200 19 works the south end of the A Yard at Shops in October 1967. In the mid-1960's the C&IM added modern roller-bearing equipped wheel-sets and full length handrails to the car-body of all six SW1200's. The drop step on the frame was elevated to match the height of an SD9. This feature came in handy when the SW1200's assisted the SD9's in road service. Engine 19 was the first diesel to leave the roster. It was sold to Commonwealth Edison in October 1979, replacing an aging SW1 at the Powerton Generating Station. *(Terry Cook)*

RIGHT - The C&IM placed two orders for SW1200's in 1955. Delivered in November together with the five SD9's, the second order included four engines numbered 20-23. SW1200 20, the first unit of the second order, switches the Havana Yard on January 26, 1971. Veteran conductor Myrl "Shep" Daniels hops aboard as engine 20 makes a switching move toward the dumper. The second order of SW1200's differed from the first order in two ways. The cabs roofs on 20-23 were painted green instead of black. They also were built with dual-cab controls, instantly recognizable by the rearward facing horn on the cab roof. The C&IM later added a canvas tarp for the radiator screen and bent-screen spark arrestors crafted by the machinists in the Springfield Diesel Shop. *(Railscene by Steve Rippeteau)*

ABOVE - SW1200 21 sits, literally, at the end of the line as she suns herself at Taylorville awaiting a call to duty in March 1968. SW1200's 20-23 were delivered without the lower window on the fireman's side of the cab. Engine 21 will handle all of the switching and transfer work on the Taylorville Division. It's hard to believe that one little diesel could replace a small army of 0-8-0's and 2-10-2's that once powered the yard jobs and mine runs on the Taylorville Division.
(Terry Cook)

RIGHT - Nearly one month after the take-over by Genesee & Wyoming, unit 22 sits on the west running track at the Diesel Shop on March 3, 1996 wearing the final paint scheme displayed by the SW1200's. When the SW1200's were repainted in the 1980's, the original 8" red and white stripe was replaced by a 6" stripe made of 3M reflective material. The herald on the cab was a smaller version of the traditional herald, which came from an order of decals designed for the company pick-up trucks. Engine 21 was the only SW1200 not repainted into this scheme. Unique to unit 22 were the tractor-style exhaust caps, which were counter-balanced to close when the engine was shut down.
(Richard Ward)

RIGHT - On September 16, 1976 freshly re-painted SW1200 23 switches cars at the south end of the B Yard in Springfield. During the mid-1970's all of the SW1200's were re-painted into a simplified paint scheme. The stripe was omitted and green replaced the black on the cab roof. The handrails, step edges, hand holds and coupler cut levers were painted a bold orange. Interestingly, in this view, the back of the steps on the unit are open, but in later years they were boxed-in with sheet metal.
(Don Woodworth Collection)

LEFT - In 1959 the Midland placed an order for the only RS1325 road switchers built by EMD. Assigned road numbers 30 and 31, they had the cab/nose assembly of a GP20 and a lengthened (by 18" next to the cab) long hood of an SW1200. The RS1325's had tiny number boards on the cab, unlike the larger number boards normally found on a GP20 or an SD18. The units originally had a black roof and an eight-inch red and white stripe. Delivered with dual-cab controls and flexi-coil road trucks, the RS1325's cost $148,135 each. Except for a few minor details these units were maintained in as-built appearance until repainted in 1984. *(Dave McKay, Morning Sun Books Collection)*

LEFT - RS1325 30 sits between two road units at Springfield on October 18, 1975. Ordered to assist SD9's and SW1200's on coal trains, mine runs, and switch jobs, engine 30 was delivered to the C&IM on October 3, 1960. When built, the radiator fan housing was painted white. The shops added a three-pane all-weather window and an immersion heater receptacle located on the car body above the stripe near the two rear hood doors. Both RS1325's had a rear head light/number board housing that was custom crafted by EMD. No other EMD locomotives were built with this type of housing. *(Richard Ward)*

ABOVE - RS1325 31 sits in front of the Diesel Shop in Springfield awaiting the 5:30PM Shops Roadswitcher crew on Saturday, September 22, 1990. The 31 was delivered to the Midland on October 24, 1960. Repainted in 1984, the 30 and 31 were the only units in the railroad's history without the 18 inch C-&-I-M initials on the long hood. While the 31's exhaust stacks were painted black, the 30 retained green stacks. Other modifications included the removal of the foot boards and the addition of extensions to the coupler cut levers. The C&IM originally equipped all road units with a Commander mechanical beacon in the mid-1970's, but later fitted them with a solid state electrical beacon in 1987. The RS1325's were the last road units to be fitted with a head end receiver for operation of a rear of train telemetry device.

(James Lewnard)

RIGHT - The C&IM ordered five SD9's in 1955. Assigned numbers 50-54, they were delivered along with SW1200's 20-23. SD9 50 displays a modified paint scheme at Springfield on August 14, 1971. Around 1963 the shop forces repainted the black portions of the carbody green. The SD9's were delivered with a winterization hatch over the first radiator fan. Engine 50, the first SD9 delivered, made its maiden voyage on November 17, 1955 with a Peoria Turn from Shops, consisting of 63 loads and five empties. It returned to Shops the following day pulling 17 loads and 76 empties.

(James Lewnard Collection)

RIGHT - SD9 52 lays over at the Diesel Shop proudly displaying its 19 year-old EMD stripe design on August 19, 1974. The SD9's were once the premier coal power on the Midland, but by this date SD38-2's 70-75 have replaced the SD9's as the front line power. Around 1974 the SD9's and SD18's were fitted with an unusual air filtration system on the long hood, nick-named "elephant ears." Assembled by the shop machinists at Springfield, the air filters replaced the original oil bath filters. C&IM machinists say that oil bath filters actually worked better, but the paper air filters were easier to maintain.

(David G. Kimmel, Tom Ratsch Collection)

ABOVE - SD9 53 sits at Shops awaiting a call to duty on May 22, 1966. The shop forces have added a fire cracker antenna to the middle of the cab roof that enabled crews to use two-way radios. The SD9's had an average working weight of 372,227 pounds, which made them exceptional pullers. Unit 53 was repainted twice by the Midland, once in the solid green scheme and again in the lightning stripe scheme in December of 1994. The SD9's lasted well beyond the take-over by Genesee & Wyoming. Interestingly, not one C&IM diesel was ever scrapped by the Midland, and only unit 51 was officially retired and used for parts. The four active SD9's were stored during the 1980's. Unit 54 made a run on October 19, 1984 before it joined the other three. In January 1989, 52 and 54 were the first SD9's to return to service when they were leased to the Chicago, Missouri & Western. *(James Lewnard Collection)*

RIGHT - In all its glory, SD9 54 sits at the Springfield Diesel Shop on November 10, 1961. This is the original factory lightning stripe scheme applied by EMD in 1955. Until 1963 the top of the SD9's were painted black. The black atop the hood curved down approximately seven inches onto the sides of the car body. The black along the bottom of the access panels was also seven inches wide. In this view there is no bell between the exhaust stacks because the original placement for the bell was behind the fuel tank between the frame rails.
(Emery Gulash, Morning Sun Books Collection)

ABOVE - In 1974 management decided to repaint the SW1200's and SD9's in the plain green scheme displayed by recently repainted SD9 54 at Springfield on July 2, 1975. During the repainting process, the green was spray painted, but the white lettering was stenciled and hand painted by the carmen who had learned the trade from the steam era guys in the paint shop. A stencil was held up with tape, and chalk was blown on the outline of the character. Once this was done, the white paint was applied with a brush. The repaints in the 1980's utilized spray cans of white enamel to speed up the painting process. *(Don Woodworth)*

ABOVE - In 1992 the C&IM repainted three units in a dark green scheme that included white adhesive-backed vinyl numbers and letters. At Springfield on September 30, 1997, SD9 54 appears in its final paint scheme. On the SD9's the letters C-&-I-M were set back on the carbody below the radiator screens to ease the application of the lettering. The access hatches along the frame were all black on both sides. In the 1990's, the mechanical beacon was replaced with a solid state electrical unit. Of the four active SD9's, 50 was the only unit not repainted a third time. *(James DuBose, Ryan Crawford Collection)*

ABOVE - SD18 60 heads up an engine consist at Shops in September 1968. The C&IM ordered two SD18's from EMD and assigned them road numbers 60 and 61. SD18 60 was built by EMD in December 1961, and was delivered by the GM&O on the 17th of the month. The following day it handled a Short Turn to Ellis and back.

C&IM SD18's were built using a low-nose SD24 car body. The only SD18's built without dynamic brakes, the C&IM units have a uniquely shaped hood that replaced dynamic brake grids. Both SD18's came with a winterization hatch covering the forward radiator fan.

(Terry Cook)

LEFT - SD18 61 and SD38-2 72 sit at North St. Louis yard working off horsepower hours owed to the BN on October 12, 1980. SD18 61 arrived on the Midland in June of 1962. The SD18's operated in their original paint scheme for nearly 25 years. By this time the shop has added some equipment. A bracket type bell has been added between the exhaust stacks, replacing the SP-style bell that was originally located atop the hood directly behind the cab. The Midland also added a Commander mechanical beacon to the cab roof, and elephant ears to the car body. The footboards have been removed and extensions added to the coupler cut levers. The 61 has a 48" flat-top radiator fan that differed from the 60's pan-top fan. *(Mike Wise, Don Woodworth Collection)*

LEFT - Two months after being released from the paint shop, SD18 61 sits quietly at Springfield Shops on October 3, 1987. The 60 was repainted in the summer of 1985 and 61 was repainted in August of 1987. The average working weight of the SD18's was 371,556 lbs, which was actually less than the SD9's. As was the norm, both of the SD18's were built with dual cab controls. *(Rick Conrath, Ryan Crawford Collection)*

ABOVE - SD38-2 71 shares the west running track with SD9 54 at Shops on November 13, 1984. The six C&IM SD38-2's were built on the same 68' 10" frame used on EMD's SD40-2. They had normally aspirated 645 engines that generated 2,000 h.p., a 3,200 gallon fuel tank, an 81-inch nose and dual cab controls. They were the first engines on the Midland to be equipped with a head end receiver, allowing them to use a F.R.E.D. (flashing rear end device). This move coincided with the CNW's system wide plan to utilize a rear end device in place of cabooses in 1987. The 71 has lost its foot boards and has a mechanical beacon atop its cab. The beacons on the 70 series engines were mounted on a plate about eight inches above the cab roof. *(Railscene by Steve Rippeteau)*

ABOVE - SD38-2 71 sits in its original paint scheme at Shops on October 18, 1975. When the SD38-2's were built in 1974 they were delivered to the C&IM without a herald on the rear of the car-body. The C&IM added this shortly after delivery. Originally the road number on the fireman's side was not centered under the company medallion because the middle latch interfered with the paint stencils. When repainted in the 1980's the SD38-2's had 14¼ inch numbers centered under the medallion on both sides, but did not have a herald on the rear of the long hood. A close inspection reveals the immersion heater receptacle above the rear truck near the jacking pad. *(Richard Ward)*

ABOVE - SD18 61 is handling the Expediter duties on June 6, 1992, as she tows badly damaged 72 out of the East Peoria Yard at Wesley. The previous day, 72 was heading north on the P&PU mainline with a three-car Expediter when it hit a semi tractor-trailer carrying steel beams. Engineer Charlie McQuern and conductor Myrl Daniels hit the deck as the 72's long hood took the brunt of the collision. The fuel tank was punctured and spilled nearly 200 gallons of diesel fuel. The Midland extensively rebuilt the long hood with a shell from a former Chessie unit and completely repainted it at Springfield. The only C&IM SD38-2 to be repainted twice, the 72 received a new scheme that was similar to the dark green found on SD9's 52 and 54. Although vinyl lettering was added, it no longer had a herald on the nose. *(Steve Smedley, Ryan Crawford Collection)*

ABOVE - On October 4, 1994 SD38-2 72 sits at Ilmo, Missouri during its second lease to the SP. The SD38-2's will never return to the C&IM. Leased to the SP from April of 1993 until January 1995, they were sold to the UP to raise much-needed cash. This created a motive power crisis. The C&IM resurrected the SD9's and pulled the SW1200's out of storage. The railroad once again operated with its original 1960's motive power.
(Mike Wise, Ryan Crawford Collection)

LEFT - On June 2, 1974, nearly new SD38-2 74 suns herself outside of the Diesel Shop at Springfield. The SD38-2's were delivered from EMD in May of 1974 and bore road numbers 70-75. They came from the factory painted green with orange handrails and grab irons. Within two years the edges of the steps and foot boards were painted orange. Engine 74 was the heaviest of the 70 class engines, weighing in at 394,499 lbs. This was 10 tons heavier than the heaviest SD9.
(Richard Wallin)

LEFT - Considered the perfect engine for the C&IM, the SD38-2's were versatile units that did not sit still for long periods of time. After delivery they were mixed with SD9's and SD18's in four-unit road sets out of Springfield. These sets could handle 60-car Monterey coal trains from Barr up Petersburg Hill without doubling. The SD38-2's also handled Short Turns and were later used in three-unit sets on the unit coal trains. In later years the SD38-2's also handled the Expediter and occasional heavy garbage traffic to the landfill. SD38-2 75, shown here, lays over with other coal power at the diesel fueling facility in March 1975.
(Richard Ward)

ABOVE - In January 1995, C&IM sold SD38-2's 70-75 to Union Pacific. In December 1995 the C&IM purchased SD20's 80-84 to alleviate the motive power crisis. Originally Southern SD24's that had been rebuilt by ICG's Paducah Shop with a low nose and a non-turbocharged 16 cylinder engine, they were overhauled by VMV's Paducah shop for C&IM service. All of the SD20's had a four-exhaust manifold and a bell on the side of the long hood. Springfield, February 24, 1996. *(Scott Muskopf)*

LEFT - Recently delivered SD20's 83 and 82 sit outside the Diesel Shop six days before the sale of the C&IM on February 3, 1996. Of the five SD20's acquired by the C&IM, only 83 had flat-top radiator fans on the long hood. The 80's were immediately put to work hauling Utah coal to Kincaid. They were also assigned to the Powerton Roadswitcher and the extra freights between Shops and Powerton. *(Richard Ward)*

LEFT - On March 9, 1996, SD20 84 sits on the Sicily siding. The SD20's displayed several unique characteristics. They were the only C&IM diesels to have snow plows and the only road units to have a single control stand. They were the only C&IM units delivered with ditchlights. Their number boards had black numbers on a white background. The SD20's had an anti-climber on the front instead of a drop step and all five had a nose headlight. The short hood of Engine 84 was longer than the other SD20's.
(Richard Ward)

117

C&IM CABOOSES AND FREIGHT EQUIPMENT

ABOVE - Rebuilt in April of 1959 following a fire that severely damaged its carbody, caboose 34 sits at Shops Yard on May 2, 1970. It was one of the last C&IM cabooses to carry the older style caboose trucks that bore a strong resemblance to a passenger car truck. Called the tramp caboose by C&IM's crews, the 34 spent its remaining years assigned to the Springfield yard jobs.
(Owen Leander, Joe Lewnard Collection)

ABOVE - Repainted red, transfer caboose 34 continued to serve at Springfield until it was cornered and flipped over in the yard. Severely damaged, it was retired.
(Thomas Hoffman, Ryan Crawford Collection)

RIGHT - C&IM 47 was one of several steel sheathed cars rebuilt from the 30-47 series cars just before WWII. Trains crews frequently prepared their meals and slept in their cabooses when away from their home terminals. The rebuilt cars included berth seats that converted into beds for four men, as well as a refrigerator, sink, stove and work table. Havana, March 1968. *(Terry Cook)*

RIGHT - C&IM 65 caboose at Ellis. In the early 1940's the C&IM rebuilt several 60 series cabooses from wooden cars carrying the same number. The cupolas were moved from the A end of the car to the center and the side windows were moved to accommodate the rebuilt interiors. In later years several of the rebuilt cars were repainted with red and white safety stripes on the ends. August 2, 1973.
(Railscene by Steve Rippeteau)

ABOVE - A trainman climbs aboard C&IM caboose 67 at Springfield Shops in June of 1960. In 1953 sixteen cabooses were required to cover the daily assignments. In 1953 the C&IM had 26 cabooses available for service, but by 1959 the number had been reduced to 16. *(Emery Gulash, Morning Sun Books Collection)*

LEFT - Cabooses 70, 65, and 63 stand in line at Shops on May 2, 1970. C&IM's rebuilt 60-70 series cabooses were repainted dark green with a red stripe after WWII. The car ends were painted solid red. The steps were painted safety yellow. The roofs were black. In the late 1950's several cabooses received safety stripes on their ends. Radios were added in the mid-1960's. *(Owen Leander, Ryan Crawford Collection)*

119

ABOVE - Recently delivered cabooses 74, 72 and 71 hold down the Cab Track at Springfield with veteran caboose 47, on September 9, 1972. The Midland purchased four modern extended cupola cabooses from International Car Company in 1972. Constructed at the company's Kenton, Ohio plant, they were assigned numbers 71-74. Utilitarian in design, they were painted green with white numbers, red chevrons and a company herald under the cupola. They were delivered with a firecracker antenna and *very* small marker lights on the end roof overhang. Caboose 72 made its final revenue run on an Extra North from Shops on Tuesday, August 15, 1989. Cabooses 71 and 72 were donated to Knights Action Park (a frequent company picnic location) in 1990 for use as party rooms. *(Railscene by Steve Rippeteau)*

RIGHT - Caboose 75 represents the second order of modern cabooses on the Midland as it brings up the rear of Extra 51 North at Ridgely, in March of 1975. Built in 1974, cabooses 75 and 76 were identical to 71-74 and were also built at International Car Company's, Kenton, Ohio plant. The last cabooses the C&IM ever purchased, the 75 and 76 were painted a darker green, which was virtually unnoticeable unless a caboose from the first and second order sat side by side. Caboose 75 made its final run in revenue service on Thursday, October 5, 1989, trailing Extra 75 North. When cabooses were used by the Extra North in 1989, they were often set out at Havana. A F.R.E.D. then replaced the caboose for the trip to East Peoria and return. Renumbered 275, it was placed on static display adjacent to the Pekin depot on July 25, 1994. *(Richard Ward)*

RIGHT - In 1990 computerization took over the Midland. The new system's switch list and way-billing programs couldn't tell the difference between the 70-series SD38-2's and the 70-series cabooses. So, what was the railroad to do? Renumber all of the cabooses into the 270 series. On April 22, 1994 at Shops, Caboose 273 has retained its as-built appearance except for the addition of a Commander mechanical beacon, back-up safety whistles on the roof, and an eight-inch red marker light. Caboose 273 made its last revenue run (as cab 73) trailing the 10:55PM Yard job from Shops to Barr and returned on Wednesday, April 12, 1989.

(James DuBose, Ryan Crawford Collection)

LEFT - In 1954 the C&IM decided to modernize its box car fleet. In the post-WWII era the C&IM leased 454 composite box cars from the Mather Humane Stock Transportation Company. Since the C&IM normally handled or held on line an average of 300 box cars a day, it was required to provide approximately the same number of cars for use in the national freight car pool. Pullman Standard provided the first 150 cars, which were delivered in July of 1954 wearing C&IM's attractive green with red stripe scheme. Numbered 16001-16150, the Pullman PS1 cars were 40' 50-ton cars with 6' Superior doors. The PS1's served in until the early 1970's. Repainted without the red stripe and herald, and renumbered as work service car X120, one of the last C&IM PS1's sits at Havana in the late summer of 1985, waiting for an occasional move in company service. *(Terry Cook)*

LEFT - In 1955 the C&IM added one hundred-fifty 40' box cars, which were built by American Car and Foundry. Numbered 16501-16650, the ACF cars had Youngstown doors and Dreadnaught ends. Painted in the green and red striped scheme with the bold C&IM lettering, they wandered the United States and Canada in general service. Often not returning to the home shop for years, they gradually lost their red stripes and traditional heralds. Sitting in back of the car shop in the summer of 1968, box car 16528 awaits the attention of the repair crew. *(Terry Cook)*

ABOVE - In July of 1960 C&IM 40' boxcars 500 and 501 sit on the Springfield Rip Track #4. Although superficially similar to the 8000 series Mather box cars the C&IM leased for many years, the two car series are different in every dimension except the width of the door (6 ft.). The 500 series cars appeared on the roster after the Mather lease expired in July of 1956. Numbered 500 to 506, they were 40' long with a 40-ton capacity. Rebuilt from older composite cars, they retain their wood doors. Unlike the Mather cars, which were painted a distinctive bright yellow, the 500's carried C&IM's more dignified dark green and red striped scheme. The cars were used for LCL service to local stations along the mainline. *(Emery Gulash, Morning Sun Books Collection)*

ABOVE - C&IM 6077 34' 2 bay hopper. In 1921 the C&IM began a modernization of its hopper car fleet with the purchase of the 6500 series 30' steel sided two bay hoppers with a 50-ton capacity. By 1931, even though the Great Depression had shattered many of the nation's businesses, the continuing need for coal deliveries to commercial customers necessitated the addition of smaller cars suitable to their needs. Since the C&IM's 7000 series gondolas were ill-suited for commercial coal service, the C&IM purchased 200 34' two-bay offset side hopper cars, numbered in the 6000 series. Essentially similar in design to the AAR standard two-bay hopper, the 6000 series could be seen all across the Midwest delivering coal. The 6000 series carried C&IM distinctive large lettering throughout their service lives. By 1941 the C&IM rostered 350 cars in the 6000 series. *(Terry Cook)*

ABOVE - C&IM 7571 70-ton gondola. Shortly after the purchase of the Springfield to Peoria mainline (1927), the C&IM acquired three hundred-fifty 70-ton solid-bottom gondolas for coal service. By 1940 there were 1,000 gondolas in the 7000 series. Built primarily to deliver coal to the Havana transfer, they were unloaded in a rotary car dumper. Lacking bottom hoppers or drop-bottom doors, they were less likely to be used in interchange service with other railroads than the 6000 series cars. The 7000 series gondolas formed the core of the C&IM's fleet of coal cars. They were supplemented by 500 wood-sided 50-ton gondolas in the 5000 series and one hundred 40-ton steel gondolas in the 9000 series leased from the Mather Car Company.

(Terry Cook)

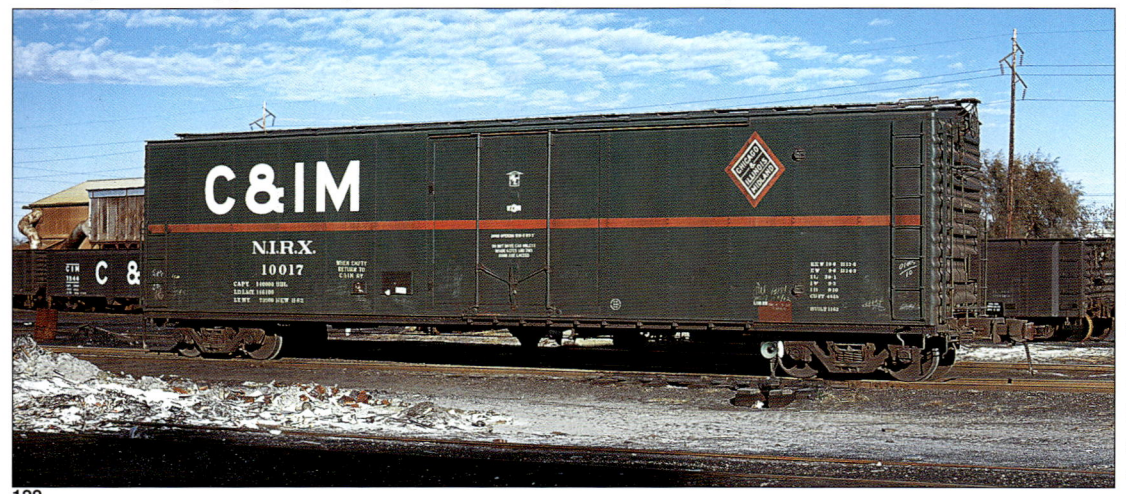

LEFT - To handle the many grocery products that Pillsbury shipped from Springfield, the C&IM leased eight North American Car Company 70-ton plug door boxcars. One of these cars, NIRX 10017, is shown at Springfield in March of 1968. These cars were equipped with loading devices and cushion under frames to prevent damage en route. They were built in November 1962, and were painted all green with a six-inch red stripe and huge billboard letters. These cars had a single plug door with a capacity of 4,618 cubic feet *(Terry Cook)*

ABOVE - C&IM's most modern box cars sit on the Team Track at Shops in February 1987. In 1974, the Midland purchased six Pullman Standard boxcars with a capacity of 5,277 cubic feet. These XM class cars were painted green with a galvanized roof and numbered 1001-1006. They were used for hauling grain and general purpose loading for Pillsbury. They were stored longer than they were used and were eventually sold to the San Luis Central Railway in 1990. *(Terry Cook)*

ABOVE - The 4,000 cubic foot Thrall unit train gondola was synonymous with C&IM coal operations after 1971. The Midland amassed a fleet of nearly 1,000 of these rotary coupler equipped cars. The first group of Thrall cars was purchased by the railroad in 1971, assigned to the 8000-8553 number block. CIM 8248 displays its original paint scheme on the rip track at Springfield on October 2, 1989. Note the repainted C-I-M, which is bigger than the original lettering from the factory. *(Roger Bee)*

ABOVE - Commonwealth Edison also purchased many Thrall-built coal gondolas for unit train service starting in 1964. The early Thrall design had tube-steel bracing that was very difficult to fit and weld. Later cars were built with I-beam braces that were much stronger. The early cars had more angled ends and sides, and lacked horizontal end braces running to the second vertical brace. Several of these cars were acquired secondhand from Com Ed and were numbered in the 9000 series. At Springfield on May 10, 1995, a former Com Ed Thrall car, CIM 9600, shows its age with more angled ends and a lack of lengthened end bracing. This car represents the highest numbered Thrall car in the fleet and the last Thrall gondola painted at Springfield in March of 1992. *(Ryan Crawford)*

123

ABOVE - Longtime C&IM conductor Dallas Stout provides protection for an unusual shoving move into Shops Yard on November 26, 1995. Conductor Stout is riding on CIM 9535, a 9000 series C&IM Thrall gondola of the newer design with the lengthened end braces and I-beam side braces. Most of C&IM's 9000 series Thrall cars were of the older design, but there are always exceptions to the rule! A longtime contract between Com Ed and the C&IM stipulated that the carrier have at least 200 protection coal cars for Commonwealth Edison's needs. The Midland's coal cars were frequently leased to the Rio Grande, Wheeling & Lake Erie and several utility companies in later years.
(James Lewnard)

RIGHT - In the late 1970's the Midland acquired 250 used coal hoppers to supplement its huge fleet of Thrall gondolas. Built by Bethlehem Steel for Peabody Coal Company, they originally had reporting marks PCCX, and were numbered 300-549. They had a capacity of 4,000 cubic feet and were equipped with a rotary coupler. The C&IM purchased these cars and assigned them to the lease pool and the western unit coal train pool. CIM 477 sits outside the Paint Shop at Springfield in August 1986 in a fresh coat of black and white. This solid white end scheme also found its way onto some Thrall gondolas. These hoppers originally wore an all-black scheme with a white vertical stripe on the first rib and a white horizontal stripe wrapped around its rotary end. *(James DuBose)*

RIGHT - CIM 5654, a Pullman Standard rotary coal gondola, sits with other C&IM unit train cars in CNW's Council Bluffs, Iowa yard on December 3, 1994. These were formerly Commonwealth Edison 5500-5799, which were purchased and re-stenciled by the C&IM in the late 1980's. They had a capacity of 4,000 cubic feet and a red rotary end. They were built in June of 1975 at Pullman's Butler, Pennsylvania plant. For a while these cars were leased to Northern Indiana Public Service Company and were mixed with their yellow and black Thrall gondolas hauling coal from the Freeman Crown Mine III at Farmersville on the Illinois Central. *(Roger Bee)*

ABOVE - Beginning in October 1957, the C&IM converted three Pullman-Standard 50-ton hoppers into covered hoppers for company sand service. Numbered 2001, 2002 and 2005, they were painted in this eye-catching livery with a green body, bold white letters, six-inch red stripe and medallion. They were rebuilt with six round loading hatches, reconditioned 70-ton trucks, new hopper bottoms and interior liners for air-aided unloading. When rebuilt, they were fitted with a quick-connect coupling that forced the sand into the tower. Having a capacity of 2,215 cubic feet, 2001 straddles the unloading pit at the Springfield servicing facility in June 1960. This car handled its first load of locomotive silica sand from Wedron, Illinois (CB&Q) on October 22, 1957. *(Emery Gulash, Morning Sun Books Collection)*

LEFT - Typical of the financially conscious C&IM in the 1970's and 80's, the sand cars were repainted black as typified by 2005 at Springfield on June 11, 1990. This car was repainted in July 1981 and had a capacity of 2,133 cubic feet. It was assigned to Havana for much of its life. The third sand car, 2002 was the "roamer" serving Taylorville and Powerton. It's interesting that the Midland only built three sand cars to serve four diesel servicing locations. *(James DuBose)*

ABOVE - Late in its career, steam wrecker X32 sits at Shops in 1977. Built in 1927 by Bucyrus Company with a builder number of 4977, it had a lifting capacity of 150 tons. Its coal bunker held 2,500 lbs and its water tank held 575 gallons. X32 was C&IM's "jack-of-all-trades" crane for 51 years. Aside from handling wrecker duties for the C&IM, it was frequently called upon by other railroads in the region to assist with their clean-ups and re-railing. It was also used for lifting prime movers into and out of diesels. After being the last steam-operated piece of equipment on the railroad, X32's fire was permanently dropped in 1978. In that same year it was donated to the Monticello Railway Museum where it still resides. *(Railscene by Steve Rippeteau)*

ABOVE - In May of 1965 C&IM crane X32 assists Illinois Terminal's wrecker X30 in cleaning up a derailment at Tansey interlocking on the south side of Springfield. The Illinois Terminal crossed the B&O's Springfield Branch at Tansey. *(Richard Wallin)*

RIGHT - On May 2, 1970, maintenance-of-way steam crane X-41 and Bucyrus steam wrecker X-32 sit idle next to the Blue Room (company meeting room) awaiting a call to duty. The X-41 had a large clam shell bucket which was used for cleanup work and rip-rap loading. This crane also had a huge pile-driving apparatus which attached to its crane boom for building and maintaining C&IM's multitude of wooden bridges. Boom car X-85 started life as a wooden coal gondola, which was later rebuilt with steel side sheets. Beneath the cab number, a safety slogan says: *"Safe Operation Prevents Injury."* *(Owen Leander, Ryan Crawford Collection)*

RIGHT - Diesel powered crane X46A sits with its boom car X46B at Springfield on June 25, 1995. X46A was supposed to replace X-32, but it didn't quite fill the bill. It was purchased second-hand from a rock quarry in Indiana, but was rarely used. The diesel shop personnel used this crane to lift locomotive hoods. Boom car X46B, formerly boom car X85, was used for a while with steam crane X41. This car has been modified with cut-out ends to accommodate X46A's lower boom height. This crane was sold shortly after the takeover by the Genesee & Wyoming. *(Paul Fries)*

LEFT - In the 1950's the C&IM rostered five hundred 41' outside braced wooden coal gondolas numbered 5000-5499. Their hard life in coal service made them candidates for rebuilding by the Taylorville shops. Most were scrapped, but a few were rebuilt with steel side sheets for MOW material service and boom-car service. They handled ties and rail as well as other miscellaneous loads. C&IM X92 sits on the Cimic Siding on March 9, 1996. Incredibly, a few of these cars still exist on the Illinois & Midland, and can be found anywhere on the line from Pekin to Taylorville.
(Don Woodworth)

ABOVE - Every railroad has their oddball equipment, and the C&IM was no different. This low sided gondola, CIM RY X75, sits on one of the Springfield Rip Tracks on April 7, 2007. Not much is known about this M-of-W car other than it is unique. The carmen say X75 was used for hauling rail, ties and other miscellaneous track components. *(Ryan Crawford)*

LEFT - The C&IM had seven modern ballast hoppers similar to C&IM 2054 at Shops on May 10, 1995. These cars started life as 70-ton covered hoppers, and were rebuilt by the carmen at Springfield in the late 1970's. During the rebuild they were fitted with rotating gate doors and new end/top sheets. They were numbered 2050-2056 and wore this all-black scheme. The full C-&-I-M lettering was rare for in-service cars at this late date. Not all of the ballast hoppers were alike, and they all had different capacities. C&IM 2054 had a capacity of 2,003 cubic feet. *(Ryan Crawford)*

RIGHT - C&IM X117 bunk car sits at Shops on May 2, 1970. This former GM&O coach was assigned to the wreck train in the mid-1960's. It currently resides at the Illinois Railway Museum at Union, Illinois.
(Owen Leander, Joe Lewnard Collection)

ABOVE - C&IM business car 90 sits in the car shops at Springfield in June of 1960. Built as a wooden coach by the St. Charles Car Company in 1890 for the Chicago, Peoria, and St. Louis, #90 was rebuilt for use as a business car by 1900. The C&IM purchased the car from William Hurst in 1928 and rebuilt it with a steel frame and car sides in the Taylorville Shops in 1929. The C&IM used the car primarily for inspection trips. When not in use it was stored at Springfield with a large canvas tarp protecting its open platform. By 1963 the 90 was rarely used and it was sold. For several years it sat near the Soo Line engine house in Schiller Park, Illinois. Later it was moved to the Mid-Continent Railway Museum in North Freedom Wisconsin, where it is displayed today.
(Emery Gulash, Morning Sun Books Collection)

RIGHT - Four months after the C&IM discontinued passenger service, coach 401 sits at Springfield Shops. Built by Pullman as a part of lot 6104 in 1927, there were three coaches numbered 400-402. The coach's distinctive carbody and ends were essentially identical to a series of coaches built for the Chicago, South Shore, and South Bend, which was a sister company in the Insull empire. *(Richard Wallin Collection)*